Not Your Mom's Divorce

Michelle Moore, Ph.D.

Not Your Mom's Divorce

Urano
publishing
Argentina - Chile - Colombia - Spain
USA - Mexico - Peru - Uruguay

© 2023 by Michelle Moore, Ph.D.

© 2024 by Urano Publishing, an imprint of Urano World USA, Inc

8871 SW 129th Terrace Miami FL 33176 USA

Urano
publishing

Cover art and design by Sandra de Waard

Cover copyright © Urano Publishing, an imprint of Urano World USA, Inc

The first edition of this book was published in February 2024

ISBN: 978-1-953027-32-0

E-ISBN: 978-1-953027-34-4

Printed in Colombia

Library of Cataloging-in-Publication Data

Moore, Michelle

1. Family & Relationships 2. Self-care

Not Your Mom's Divorce

Foreword

Dear Reader,

It's a surreal experience, sitting down to write this foreword. For starters, it's an incredible honor. Seeing that this book is a real and tangible thing that you are lucky enough to hold in your hands, feels both heart-warming and exciting, nearly beyond words. You see, before this book was a reality, it was a process, a thought, an idea, and a collection of conversations and shared experiences, both personal and professional.

Let's back up and get to know each other a little... In May of 2006, I tied the knot to my now ex-husband. I was 23, he was 24. A few months later, we packed up our lives and moved to Southern California. I started working in the mental health field for a treatment center and eventually got promoted to an outreach role. Part of my job in this new role was to connect with mental health providers to share about the center I worked for, and to get to know them as a resource for our clients leaving treatment. That's how I first met Michelle—she was one of the first providers I had the fortune of meeting with. As a well-respected psychotherapist in her field, I was in awe at how down to earth and relatable she is. It instantly made sense to me how and why she is so successful in the work she does. Not only were we professional colleagues, we almost instantly became friends.

By 2014 though, things had changed for me a bit. At that time, I was eagerly awaiting a notice from the State of California letting me know my divorce was *finally* final. Seven days before my 31st birthday, the notice arrived and after the relief and excitement wore off, the illusion I was done with my divorce was shattered. Little did I know at the time, that simply because the state gave me a paper saying I was no longer legally married, that wasn't the actual end of the divorce process for me... and that tends to be the case for most women. The end is often the beginning, and that stands true for the divorce process. There's the "after-shock" of things you will still have to learn to navigate: there's dealing with the array of responses after letting people know you are newly single, figuring out how long you check the divorced box on any paperwork, navigating a name change, and all that comes with a new identity, and having to deal with the social stigma of being a divorced woman in this world. Oh, and there's the whole dating after divorce thing. At times it felt like I totally had it, and other times I felt like I was completely lost and exhausted. It felt like a million things that no one had ever talked about, or at least that I had never heard anyone talk about.

As time continued and as Michelle and I each navigated our respective divorce experiences, at some point in our numerous talks, she shared with me her desire to write a book. One that shifted the conversation and outdated social narratives about divorce—specifically about women and divorce. A resource that combined both her professional and personal experiences that could be a guide for women to support them through all the stages and phases of the divorce process. A tool to help them feel less alone, lost, overwhelmed and unsure. As she shared this with me, I couldn't help but be excited about her vision too. It was contagious. What I would have given to have such a tool and resource when going through my own divorce. Something that spoke to my actual experience and not the stuff portrayed in the media or the old social stigmas always talked about—because that wasn't my experience at all. While I had moments of sadness and grief, I didn't get depressed after my divorce. My health, mental health, and life actually improved. I wasn't the poor, sad, lonely divorced lady I always heard about. I was more empowered, made more money and was happier overall, despite the divorce process being hard. Divorce, for me, was the right choice. I have zero regrets. And, if I'm being completely honest, divorce is actually the thing that got me where I am today. It was the catalyst that showed me how strong and capable I actually am. It taught me to listen to, and trust, my gut—though that is still more of a work in progress, and not a perfect thing for me. Going through a divorce made clear to me that I, in fact, can do hard things... and I will survive.

The strength, wisdom and growth I gained during, through and on the other side of divorce prepared me for another hard thing I decided to do—start a business. Three years after I got those papers from the State of California, I started my coaching company. Throughout my years working in the mental health field, I discovered I had a real passion and knack for guiding and supporting mental health and other healing professionals in their own careers—particularly assisting them in establishing, growing, and thriving in their own private practices. While the coaching work I do revolves mostly around marketing, setting rates and charging for a service, at times I also get to walk others through a small part of their experience with divorce. Things like, how to navigate a name change when you have built a reputation based on a name you no longer are keeping, supporting my clients as they start letting their professional circle know, and reminding them to allow themselves some grace through it all. Divorce taught me to see the strength I have and it has allowed me the opportunity to, sometimes, help those I work with to see the strength and tenacity they have as well.

One of the incredible things I have witnessed working as a coach and a professional in the mental health field for more than sixteen years, has been the increased movement around reducing the stigma of getting support and, in general, reducing the stigma of mental health itself. That's what Michelle is doing with this book. She is reducing the stigma of being a divorced woman. She is taking the old and outdated information we, as a society, have heard on repeat and she is sharing with you updated and more accurate information, real-life experiences, and doing it in a way that couldn't be more relatable.

Michelle has expertly crafted and created a book, actually *THE* book, that I wish I had when I was going through my own divorce. One that helps you feel less alone as you are making your way. In the following pages, Michelle not only normalizes the concept, process, decisions, practical steps and actions required to get divorced, she also validates all the other stuff that comes with the dissolution of a marriage—the tears, laughs, frustrations, the navigating newness and she skillfully addresses the social stigmas that, as a woman, you are undoubtedly going to hear and have to deal with. She guides you toward support and walks you through all of it expertly blending her professional and personal experiences. Throughout this treasure of a book, Michelle empathizes with, supports, and empowers you in ways that, right now, you might not be sure can be done.

I assure you, you are in good hands. Michelle is an amazing (and funny) human being, mom, friend, and a brilliant and gifted psychotherapist who understands it all. She has been there. With this book, she'll be there for you, even including some gentle reminders for you along the way. This book is like having a best friend, therapist, guide and support system all wrapped up in a beautiful package to be with you as you consider, go through or are on the other side of divorce. Like I said, you are lucky to have this book in your hands.

Divorce does not need to define you. But, if it's part of your journey, Michelle and this book are the perfect travel mates as you make your way.

— Cassie Gaub

For my son who constantly reminds me of the importance
of helping others.

Acknowledgements

In loving appreciation to my aunt and uncle, Bob and Edie, who were by my side from the beginning, and never stepped away. Their happily married life has always been an inspiration and one that has instilled hope throughout my life.

I'm grateful for the support and guidance of my patient and loving husband Glenn, who's kind heart and listening soul has kept me grounded along this journey.

As always, my son is the strongest source of inspiration to me, just by his presence in this world. His unconditional love is the light that keeps a sometimes "darkish world" warm and comforting. From babyhood to young adulthood, he inspires me on a daily basis.

To my mom who is an amazing writer, my stepsister who is truly a superhero in the world of women, and to my extended family who are always there to lend a listening ear, and have no problem offering their advice, solicited or otherwise.

A big thank you to Cassie Gaub, who began this writing journey with me and without her collaboration, this book would have never seen the light of day. And finally, thank you to the unfailing support of my agent, Jennifer Thompson for her endless guidance, support, and patience.

To my clients who teach me far more than I could ever teach them. I'm truly blessed to be able to do the work I do.

A special thank you to Katie Foster, my dear friend and neighbor. For without her, I would have never been able to move my couch or wiggle my Christmas tree into my car.

And to my friends and neighbors who have helped me grow, reminded me of the importance of being humble while also being proud, and who constantly remind me that their presence is an endless source of love and inspiration.

And finally, a truly special thanks to my ex-spouse, "Simon," for being the best dad I could've hoped for for my son, and a pretty damn decent ex-husband to boot. It hasn't always been easy, but he has grown as much as I have over the years, and for that, I am grateful.

Table of Contents

Introduction

When we think of the word divorce, we tend to feel sorry for "those people," especially the women. We tend to view divorced women as women who either lost a husband, or worse yet, couldn't keep him. We tend to feel pity, and as ashamed as I am to say it, I've been guilty of the same stereotypical thoughts. Until, that is, at the end of my own marriage—I wasn't going to feel sorry for myself and I was going to create a better life for myself and my son. Pity isn't an option.

When I was going through my divorce, I couldn't find one single book that would help me. Everything I read either made me want to curl up in the fetal position with my thumb in my mouth or bored me to sleep. They all seemed to categorize me as either a woman who should be enraged or crying myself to sleep. And the information provided did very little to assist with the everyday mundane divorce tasks, coupled with the sometimes-exhausting emotional roller coaster that divorce brings to the table. The goal of this book is to provide the "right information" to women out there who are, like you, somewhere on the divorce spectrum.

I started writing this book because the resources available were scarce and going through divorce first hand gave me the insight to recognize something that was so desperately needed. In sharin'g our stories with one another, we find a connection, a safe place to talk about the taboo of divorce. As humans, we find comfort and humor in sharing our stories, and our shared experiences can make life's journey, not only less bumpy, but less lonely and confusing as well. Because I work with women on a daily basis, I know women who are going through divorce are looking for answers and support, they seek it out within the four walls of our therapy rooms. My goal in writing this book is to provide them with a resource that wasn't available to me during my own divorce process, but that would have been so beneficial.

Not Your Mom's Divorce is designed to provide a combination of research, clinical expertise, and personal experience to support, guide, and educate women through the divorce process and empower them to move forward. The approach is a balance of education and vulnerability from the unique personal and professional perspectives of a psychologist/divorced woman, with a voice that is real, raw, and relatable that examines the whole experience of divorce, well beyond the emotional recovery from an ending relationship. It brings all things related to divorce, including identifying, addressing, and navigating the intricacies of the process, to the surface.

In writing this book, my goal was to create an empowered tribe of women who understand the difficulty of divorce, despite any particular circumstances, and who are tired of the "woe is me" information about divorce. A tribe of women who are tired of hearing, and feeling like they are "less than" without a relationship and who are ready to move past the victim mindset and move through their process empowered, supported, and understood.

It's time that women knew the options for happiness, better health, and just an overall more fulfilling and gratifying life that are available to them, and they don't have to stay in an unhappy, unhealthy, or unfulfilling marriage. It's time they remember their goals, rediscover their desires, and believe in their value as women, as individuals.

Regarding terminology, throughout the book, I will most often use the words "woman"/"women" and the pronouns "she"/"hers." I understand that may not necessarily be how you, as the reader, identify. My hope is that this book is as informative and inclusive as possible, and I acknowledge that there may be some gaps because of limited, personal, and professional experiences. Throughout the book, I am often sharing my personal experiences, and those of past clients and current colleagues and want to share their experiences with as much openness, honesty, and vulnerability as possible. As often as possible, I try to include evidence-based research-backed concepts and statistics. Much of that research, unfortunately, at the time of writing this book, is accumulated using cis-gendered, heterosexual parameters. My goal, hope, and intention is that this book can create discussion, connection, understanding, and community among all of us—whether cisgendered or not, whether in a straight heterosexual relationship or not.

Although writing this book was one of necessity, to provide women with the support I was lacking when I divorced, the decision to share many of the most intimate and personal details related to one of the toughest experiences of my life, wasn't one that I took lightly. I didn't want to paint a negative picture of my loved ones or my ex-husband, and I certainly didn't want to hurt anyone's feelings. That is why, in sharing my story, my goal is one of utmost transparency. Out of respect for those in my past and present life, I own my flaws, mistakes, mishaps, and flat out "fuck ups." The amazing Anne Lamott once said:

"Remember that every single thing that happened to you is yours, and you get to tell it. If people wanted you to write more warmly about them, they should've behaved better."

That rule applies to me as well.

I'm grateful for and protective of the stories of my clients that have helped create *Not Your Mom's Divorce*. Their experiences have helped bring to life a powerhouse of knowledge and empowerment on these pages. Each individual's story is the story of a "few," creating a narrative that can be familiar to many.

Throughout history, women have had to rely on the connection with other women in order to survive the toughest of times. It is often through the use of our words that we support, befriend, educate, and relate to one another. My hope is that, in reading *Not Your Mom's Divorce*, women feel supported, educated, and empowered during this very difficult time, and are provided the tools to understand their feelings, and the encouragement to keep pressing forward. We don't have to do this alone.

So, wherever you are in the process, I'm glad you're here and hope that the sharing of personal and professional experiences can be a support and inspiration to you, however you may need it.

Wait, Who's Life is This?

Divorce is part of my family history, sometimes it feels even genetic. My mom has been divorced four times, my sister, grandparents, aunt and uncle, and the majority of my first cousins have all been divorced, many more than once. I remember my first therapist telling me, "You'll never get divorced" and I wasn't even married yet. I recall saying "Yes I will!" but realizing that at 35, and not being married, maybe he had a point. The idea of getting married, and then divorced, terrified me. So, I waited and waited for the right person, the perfect person I knew for sure I would never divorce.

I met Simon when I was 35 years old, after a very long stint of graduate school. I was busy, committed to my dissertation, which is an all-consuming partner. After I graduated, at age 30, I dated and had relationships. I was what you would call a serial monoga-mist. But I didn't want to rush into marriage; I didn't wait that long to settle for the wrong guy.

We met on Match.com after I had just ended a relationship with a rather psychotic neighbor of mine and I was forced to move from Newport Beach to Brea, California. That relationship was convenient, until it wasn't. Because of that rather tumultuous rela-tionship, I had lost all interest in dating. However, my girlfriends had a different plan for me. They convinced me into joining Match.com for a 30-day trial.

On the 30th day of my free trial membership, after many un-interesting interactions, I met Simon. His picture was sweet, and I liked that he was from the Midwest—a clean-cut guy who prob-ably treated his mom like a queen and earned all of his badges in Boy Scouts. He seemed normal, and that was so important given my recent history with less than normal boyfriends, to put it mildly.

We went out, had a great time, a refreshing connection and in-stant chemistry. One date led to another, and another, and a year later were engaged. The next year we were married, and the year after that I was pregnant. It was the perfect plan, on paper.

Maybe I should've known it wasn't going to work out when he proposed. Sometimes you just have that feeling, but since it was so subtle, I just brushed that nagging feeling aside. I rationalized that feeling away by thinking, "Maybe I'm just commitment-phobic. I'm sure it's just me and I'll get over my nervousness soon enough."

Simon and I were having a picnic at the beach, and I remem-ber him asking me to pass him the mustard. As I leaned over to grab the Dijon mustard, he pulled out the ring. I clearly recall feeling shocked and blurting, "Are you kidding? Put that back!" And then I think I felt sick. I'd heard stories of women crying in utter glee and excitement or brimming with giddiness as their adoring husband-to-be popped the question, but that wasn't the feeling I felt. I felt nauseous, like the world was reeling around me, and I was scared. Although I was scared, I knew I wanted to be married, and I loved Simon. And, for a long time, we were good together. After a year of marriage, I gave birth to an amazing, beautiful baby boy. He was thrilled to be a dad, and I knew he would be good at it. But our marriage started to falter.

Simon isn't a bad guy, and I loved him, I loved him a lot, once upon a time. But we had problems. He had his problems, I had mine, and we had problems together. He had issues with chemical dependency, that I enabled or minimized, and like any addiction, it started to destroy us, as it does anyone in its path, and our life together started feeling like an emotional roller coaster. And I tried to make it work. I really tried.

I was your classic co-dependent spouse. I did everything I thought I wouldn't, said everything I thought I shouldn't, and felt quite sorry for myself along the way. That's the truth. I enabled, bitched, nagged, cried, and denied for a very long time. I was ashamed, embarrassed, and confused. We started arguing, and bickering constantly, about anything and everything. I was critical, and he was moody, and we were a mess. But still, the idea of divorce truly never entered my mind. We were married, and I was sure that our problems were no different than those that other married couples experienced and pushed through in order to preserve the sanctity of their union. Everyone in my social circle was married. There was only one single mom, and her social circle was different. I didn't want to be a single mom; I couldn't imagine that. I wouldn't let myself imagine that. I wanted to keep the life I created, I didn't want it to change, so I had to make it work.

I'm a therapist, so I'm really trying not to be a hypocrite. I don't judge my patients for divorcing, not at all. I've even condoned it at times based on their situation. But when it came to my expectations of myself and my marriage, they were sky high.

The first time the word "divorce" came up was during one of our fights about nothing, and Simon yelled, "We should just get divorced!" I was in shock. I knew he didn't mean it, but it threw me, nonetheless. Professionally, I know that when people threaten divorce in the middle of an argument, it's rarely meant to be taken seriously. It's typically the result of their own pain, insecurities, fear of abandonment, etc., that prompts this hurtful outburst. They may feel unseen and unheard by their partner, or unloved, and ultimately, emotionally unsafe. Ultimately lashing out with verbal threats of divorce is a form of relationship sabotage, a pre-emptive strike if you will. "I'll hurt me/us before you can!"

But hearing it in that moment, not only wounded me, it also scared me to death. Although I grew up amidst generations of divorce, I had never considered that an option for us. I thought we were different and that we should make it work, no matter what. Unfortunately, it wouldn't be the last time that those resounding words hit my ears. And, in a way, I felt that Simon was just crying wolf. But we were on very shaky ground, and I felt emotionally unsafe at that point. To say I was stressed would be a huge understatement. The problem with stress is that it isn't supposed to be chronic, it's rooted in our fight or flight response. Our fight or flight response is activated when our body perceives a threat, and we return to normal once the threat passes. But, if the threat doesn't pass, our body still feels like it is in danger and is on high alert. Our muscles remain contracted, our heart rate continues to stay elevated, and we continue to react to things around us rather than being mindful and present in our environment. I was reactive to Simon, who was reactive to me, which prohibited both of us from being proactive when it came to our relationship.

The day I gave myself permission to even consider divorce was the day I met my friend and colleague, Cassie for coffee. She was 20 years younger and had married her husband at the tender age of 25 years old. Her husband and mine were acquaintances, but really just knew each other through our relationship. It had been a few years since I had seen her, so we had a lot to catch up on both professionally and personally.

After hugs, and all of our "You look so good!" pleasantries, I asked about her husband. Without blinking, she said flatly, "We're divorced." I was dumbfounded. I didn't know much about their marriage, but I didn't recall hearing about any arguments between them so I couldn't fathom why they would've split up.

I didn't ask too much about the details, but she shared enough to give me the gist. Basically, he was a narcissist, was controlling and manipulative, and she just couldn't take it anymore. She told me that one day while they were sitting on their couch, he asked her to rub his feet for the millionth time, and she thought, "What the hell am I doing? I just can't do this anymore." That's when she decided. That was it. She was done. She researched how to get a divorce online, downloaded the paperwork, and filed all on her own, without a lawyer. I actually didn't know that one could do that, without a lawyer that is. I thought you needed a lawyer to draft the documents, but I was wrong. The shortened version of her story was that the whole process took 6 months, mostly because California requires you to have to wait 6 months before the divorce is finalized. They call this the "Cooling Off Period." This period of time is designed to allow you to reconsider or, at the very least, make sure this is something you want to do. After the six months were completed, her divorce was final.

As I sat there listening to her tell me her story, I realized that I too didn't have to stay in a marriage that clearly wasn't meant to work. I had never allowed myself to think about divorce until that very moment. That was the first time I had given myself permission to look at all of my options, including the one that my soon to be ex-husband had threatened on many occasions. Listening to her tell me about all of the things she had been up to, the liberating feelings she felt, I didn't feel as stuck anymore. I could do this, if I wanted to. That permission was key.

In talking to Cassie, I realized my story was not that unusual. Even if you happened to see the two of us together, you might be hard-pressed to find definitive similarities. Yet, despite our differences, we both recognized that the journey of divorce is one in which many of us share more commonalities than not. All of the struggles she faced, questions she had, and obstacles she encountered during her divorce, paralleled mine in so many ways. Moreover, both of us needed to figure out this divorce journey on our own, fumbling our way down a very unfamiliar path. Her divorce was simple, mine was complicated, yet we related on so many levels.

Through my work with clients and on my own journeys, I've learned that no matter how different we or our stories seem, much like life, even the most diverse "divorce experiences" share so many commonalities. Recognizing this reinforced the idea that, as women, and especially as women going through a divorce, we truly need to provide support, education, and empowerment to one another.

Whether you're in the contemplation stage of divorce, or well into the process, just know you're in the right place. But even in the simplest of divorces, the whole process can be difficult, ridiculous, overwhelming, and beyond confusing at times. The messages about divorce are all over the place… and it seems like they come from *everywhere* and *everyone*. You know that saying, "opinions are like assholes, everyone's got one?" It seems like when the topic of divorce comes up, opinions and assholes are abundant.

When I was going through my divorce, no one ever said to me, "Michelle, you've got this." Ironically, much of what I heard centered around the thoughts and feelings of others and their needs. I tend to teeter in the world of codependency, one in which I put the thoughts and feelings of others ahead of my own, tending to their needs before mine. But repeating this pattern at this time, especially when my needs were so critical, would've been the epitome of unhealthy. So, in writing this book, I say to you, "Not only do you 'got this,' you're also not alone." Our ability to relate, to connect, and to support one another is what gives us the strength to endure.

The Ten Rules of a Woman's Divorce

1. *You will be okay. No matter what happens, you will be just fine, in fact you might even be better.*
2. *Divorce is expensive but that's because it's worth every penny and it's impossible to put a price tag on freedom or on honoring yourself.*
3. *You're stronger and more resilient than you think.*
4. *Hold your head high so when you fall, you won't fall on your face.*
5. *Know that you will fall, over and over. Just pick yourself back up and brush yourself off.*
6. *When all else fails, find humor in the process. There will be trials and tribulations. There will also be lots to laugh at.*
7. *Don't listen to anyone's advice unless you ask for it, and preferably only if you pay for it.*
8. *Not only should you accept help but ask for it whenever possible. Remember, you are not alone or "the only one" who's gone through a divorce.*
9. *Praise yourself often, the world is better at criticism. You are always your best advocate so remember to do your job.*
10. *See rule number one.*

CHAPTER 1

The First Step: From Fear to Freedom

Life isn't easy, not by a long shot, but it can certainly be worth the effort if you believe you're worth the effort. It reminds me of the story of the Monarch butterfly. My favorite version of this story is Frank Dupree's "Metamorphosis." The story goes like this:

"A young boy came across a butterfly cocoon and brought it into his house. He watched, over the course of hours, as the butterfly struggled to break free from its confinement. It managed to create a small hole in the cocoon, but its body was too large to emerge. It was tired and became still.

Wanting to help the butterfly, the boy snipped a slit in the cocoon with a pair of scissors. But the butterfly was small, weak, and its wings crumpled. The boy expected the insect to take flight, but instead it could only drag its undeveloped body along the ground. It was incapable of flying. The boy, in his eagerness to help the butterfly, stunted its development. What he did not know was that the butterfly needed to go through the process of struggling against the cocoon to gain strength and fill its wings with blood. It was the struggle that made it stronger."

Making a change is rarely something we look forward to as human beings. We like the familiar, the safe, the comfortable, the safety of the certain. Simply put, although change is constant, we dread it, we fear it, and often resist it at all costs, and sometimes that cost can be very expensive.

I remember learning how to ski. I recall trying the patience of my instructor, over and over again, as he reminded me, at nauseum, to lean forward down "Sesame Street One—aka, the bunny hill. He insisted that if I continued to lean backward, I would inevitably fall, and it would be an ugly fall. I tried to listen. I really did, but each time I started moving I couldn't resist leaning backwards, against gravity, and consequently falling on my butt every single time. And every time I fell, it felt worse. I knew what I was doing, but I couldn't help it. I was afraid of leaning forward, it was really scary. Finally, on my 6th run, I decided "Screw it. If I'm going to die today, so be it." I took a deep breath and pushed forward. To be truthful, I didn't really lean forward but I didn't lean backward either. It wasn't graceful by any means, but I made it down that damn hill, and stayed on my two feet, barely. I remember thinking "Why did I have to make that so difficult? I know how gravity works, I'm not stupid." It made sense that I needed to lean into the direction I hoped to go... simple, right? But the logic didn't eliminate my fear of falling in that moment. And that fear felt very real.

What I realized is that falling is inevitable. We all know it, it's a no brainer. But leaning into the direction I needed to go, relying on knowledge, courage, and trust, regardless of the fear, versus leaning backward based solely on my fear of the unknown, made hitting the ground bearable, and also much easier to get back up. Plus, it hurt a whole lot less.

At various points in my life, I've recall a statement a friend once shared when referring to unwise partner choices: "I saw the red flags but thought it was a parade." That phrase came to mind when I was deciding whether or not to get divorced. I was going through my whole pros and cons list, and just overthinking everything of course. The "D" word is a no-no in my beloved town of Carlsbad by the Sea, where most people are part of a family that includes a mom, dad, and 2.2 children approximately 3 years apart in age. That was the norm, and it was expected. And let's face it, even according to William Shakespeare, unless a story has a happy ending, it's considered a tragedy.

It wasn't until I was at Disneyland, yes, the happiest place on earth, that I had an "aha" moment. I had taken my son to Disneyland and his father had accompanied us. At this point in our marriage, my husband and I were "barely tolerating one another" but staying together for the sake of our son, or so I told myself. But that day, with both of us there, I noticed that my son was not the child I knew him to be. He was agitated, moody, and disrespectful, to me specifically. I realized that our being together wasn't just a bad idea for us as husband and wife, it was a bad idea for our son. At that point I knew I was done. I don't want to make it seem like this decision was at all one I considered lightly. I hated the fact that my family would be splitting up and that my son's world was about to come crashing down. I felt like I had let everyone down, even myself. But I knew that staying together for his sake was not only going to hurt him, it would probably be the worst thing I could do as a mother.

So, at age 47, a mom with a 9-year-old son and little to no family around, I needed to end my marriage, change my life completely, and start a new chapter. How very exciting, right? Yeah, I didn't think so either.

The difficult part was having absolutely no idea what I was going to do next. I mean, they don't help you create a Plan B when two people decide to get married. The plan is to STAY married, and there's no alternative ending that provides the option of "what if it doesn't work out." My husband knew the ropes, he had been married and divorced once before. But this was all new to me, and what I did know was that I needed to be smart, for both my son and me. So, although I knew I had made the decision, it wasn't prudent to share that decision just then. I needed to learn what I didn't know; I needed to meet with an attorney.

I contacted the only other woman, or so I thought, who was divorced in my very intimate, 2.5 intact-family neighborhood. The first question out of her mouth threw me, "Do you have divorce insurance?" she asked. "I'm sorry," was my reply. "Can you repeat that?" "You know, divorce insurance," she said. But, I didn't know. And apparently, I knew even less than I thought. Who would have thought that there would be a thing called divorce insurance? She explained that divorce insurance is something that some employers offer employees as a part of their benefit package. As I was self-employed, the idea of divorce insurance never crossed my mind, especially since I considered myself a rather frugal boss. I could have kicked myself for not knowing anything about it, but alas, kicking myself would've made a stressful and complicated situation far worse. She sighed and muttered, "It's going to cost you." This was something I did know, unfortunately. She gave me the phone number of her beloved attorney, a hug, and reassured me that everything would be okay. It had to be, right? That reassurance, at that time, provided little comfort.

When I met with Sandra, this bright-eyed, feisty attorney, I was nervous, very nervous. I knew she was there to help me, but I didn't know how exactly. I remember the words of my uncle from the night before, "Do whatever she tells you to do. I don't care what it is, just do it." Umm, "ok," I thought. It sounded so dramatic, but I listened anyway. "You're paying her, so you have to listen to her, so don't be dumb." Yes, this is the warm and nurturing advice of my family during the toughest of times. Don't be dumb. Okay, I'll try really hard not to be.

So, as I sat in Sandra's office for the first time, and she asked me about my situation, I told her everything. The funny thing is that any uncertainty faded. I was no longer unsure of my decision. In fact, I don't think I could've been any surer at that exact moment. I suppose I never really allowed myself to talk openly about how unhappy I was, how just completely empty my life had been for a very long time. Sandra listened to my story, and it wasn't until I was done that she spoke. "I get it," she said. "My ex-husband was an addict." My mouth dropped. She did get it. She got it all. I listened to her story. She was a single mom raising 4 daughters all on her own. This little spitfire of a woman had done it. Maybe I could do it too.

Given the situation, she felt that it was important to file for divorce as soon as possible. Her view was that it really wasn't good to have my son around his dad while he was drinking, and I agreed.

"How long have you been married?" She asked. "Ten and half years" I sighed. And then she halted our plan. "Ummm, let's cool our heels for a second, we need to factor in the 10-year rule" she stated begrudgingly. "What's the ten-year rule?" I was confused. She seemed surprised. I guess I was too busy working and hadn't watched enough Lifetime TV to know. And so, she told me.

The ten-year rule states that if you've been married more than ten years you may be stuck paying alimony to your spouse for your entire life. Yes, forever, and ever, until the day you die. The only thing worse than that was the timeshare I'd be stuck paying for as well. And, since I was the one who worked for half of our marriage, then you guessed it, I could be screwed. "Jesus Christ!" I thought. What kind of stupid ass thought of that ridiculous law solely based on some arbitrary number? But, it didn't matter because as I was just spinning in my head, my new guardian angel was coming up with Plan B.

"Let's hold off until after Thanksgiving, just 5 days. Let me get this order into the court first and then petition for divorce." First off, let me say I really had no idea what any of that meant, but she sounded like she knew what she was talking about, and my uncle's words resonated in my head, "Don't be dumb Michelle." So, I nodded obligingly.

I remember asking Sandra so many questions, questions I felt silly asking because they felt like things I should already know. She was so patient with me, and I was grateful. I remember asking her specifically if I should move out or ask my Simon to, to which she exclaimed "Do not move out of your house! If you move out, you'll never get back in, even if you want to." I never thought of this, nor did I really know what that meant, but I listened like a good student and hung on every word.

It was at that point that I asked her pointedly what I should do for now. And she said in a very matter-of-fact tone, "You take care of that beautiful son of yours, and I'll take care of you. Remember that you're a young woman who has the rest of her life ahead of her, a future."

I couldn't believe her words. I didn't feel young, I felt old. The one thing that prevented me from moving forward for so long was the feeling that I had no choice, that I made my choice long ago and that I was too old to have another life. But she disagreed, and she was living proof.

At that moment, I pulled out every penny in my wallet and dumped out my purse on her desk. Here's everything I have. How I was going to pay for her didn't matter, I would find a way and it was the least of my concerns.

Sandra was smart as well as supportive. As we spoke, her words made an impact. She said, "Divorce, even when it's the right move for you, even if both parties are on-board or mostly on-board, is an emotional and trying process and is never 100 % smooth. Even if you come up with the best plan. But, I promise, if you trust me, it will be okay, maybe even better than that." I not only believed her and trusted her, I was starting to trust myself again. As I walked to my car, I felt better than I had in what seemed like a lifetime, or at least the past 10½ years. Damn ten-year rule.

What's next?

So, you've made your decision, now what? According to financial guru, Suzie Orman, when it comes to paying off debt, you start with the smallest loan first. You can pay off that one more quickly and gain a little momentum. According to her, momentum makes the process of moving forward far easier. And I think we could all use a little momentum, in all areas of our lives. A client of mine once said, "When faced with making a decision, the only wrong decision is to do nothing at all," and I couldn't agree more.

So, just one little step forward is really all you need to start. Try not to overthink and try not to over-plan. But do make a move before you overthink, become overwhelmed, and then feel stuck. Overthinking is the "thinking" one does when one already knows the answer. Once your mind knows the answer, the unconscious part of your brain takes over and isn't equipped to overthink, therefore it becomes quickly overwhelmed. So, before you start second-guessing a mindful choice you already made, make a move… just one, and gain a little momentum.

Often, when it comes to taking the first step most people immediately think "I can't afford to get divorced. How am I going to pay for it all?" What I learned rather quickly is that no one can ever afford to get divorced; it's not something one budgets for, unless you have the foresight to purchase divorce insurance. But even though no one can really afford to get divorced, about 50 % of the population still gets divorced, and we know the attorneys aren't doing this work pro bono.

Truthfully, you can't worry about how you're going to pay for all of it, but that's too much unnecessary thinking at one time. That's like reading *What to Expect When You're Expecting*, not as it is designed to be read, month by month, but rather in one sitting; it's way too much to process. You'll figure it out as you go. Trust yourself. You figured out how to be married, you can figure out how to get divorced. Things will work out, somehow, they always seem to. You don't need all the answers yet, but you could use a little momentum. To this day, I don't know exactly how I did it, but I did, and it wasn't as bad as I thought it would be.

Attorneys and mediators are different, their jobs differ significantly, and so do their fees. Nolo 2020 reports that the average cost of divorce mediation ranges from $3000 to $8000 with both spouses splitting the final bill. And, according to a recent survey administered by Bankrate 2020, the average cost of a divorce in the United States with both spouses hiring attorneys' is $15,000, per person. Spitzer, M. (2017) *How much does divorce cost?* Bankrate. https://www.bankrate.com/personal-finance/smart-money/how-much-does-divorce-cost/

When using the term "average," keep in mind that it really is more of a range, depending on what is needed in each case. The more involved or complicated a divorce is, the longer it may be drawn out and the more expensive it can become, for obvious reasons.

A mediator is an independent, neutral third party, representing both spouses equally, whose primary job is to help both parties identify, negotiate, and come to a mutually acceptable agreement in the dissolution of their marriage. A mediator takes an active role in the process, allowing both spouses to work together in making decisions with respect to all aspects of their divorce. A divorce attorney's role is quite different from that of a mediator. A lawyer's role is to advocate for the one party who hired them with the goal of achieving the most favorable outcome for their client.

So, how do you decide between the two? Attorney, mediator, neither, or both? Yikes! This isn't an easy decision, and much of it really depends on the level of complication you expect from the divorce process, and your ability to communicate effectively with your spouse when it comes to deciding financial issues, custody agreements, and property settlements.

There are some general "rules of thumb" criteria as well. The following situations would constitute a recommendation to hire an attorney: if there is an addiction present or your spouse is incapable of making decisions, if you believe your spouse is hiding financial assets and you need the assistance of an attorney, if your safety or the safety of your children is being threatened and being in the same room with your spouse would be dangerous or you are fearful of retaliation, or if your spouse is unwilling to participate in the mediation process.

Hiring a mediator often tends to be a little more straightforward, provided you and your spouse agree on the right person for the job. Typically, consultation appointments are complimentary, so take your time and find the right fit. You'll know when you've found the right person so trust your instincts.

When it comes to hiring a lawyer, the process can feel a little more daunting. Do your research, read reviews, ask friends, co-workers, anyone who's judgment, as well as discretion, you trust and interview the right attorney or mediator for the job. Make an appointment and be prepared to take notes.

When you decide, pay the retainer. The retainer is a lump sum the attorney requests up front in order to cover the initial expenses.

It's held in an account in your name, for your legal needs. If for some reason you change your mind, this money should be fully refundable, but do confirm reimbursement policies. Retainers are also negotiable so don't be afraid to negotiate on legal fees. Trust me, attorneys rarely, if ever, get offended.

And, after they're hired, trust them, but not beyond question. Don't be afraid to ask questions, express concerns, and share disapproval. Remember that person works for you, gets paid by you, and wouldn't have a job if it wasn't for you. But don't trust them blindly, be mindful and wise.

Attorneys also often have their hands full with other clients, so your divorce may not be at the forefront of their mind 24/7, which is something I learned early on in the process. As shocked as I was, my attorney didn't always have my file in front of her. Nor was she just sitting by her phone waiting to hear from me and catering to my every request at the drop of a hat. So, if you need answers fast, continue to do your research. And, if I learned one thing from every document signed or meeting I had, everything seems to cost exactly $800.00.

If something doesn't seem right, or if you're confused about the process, don't be afraid to bring it up. Call their office, send an email, or a text, and don't be concerned about bothering them. You'd be surprised by the clients that walk through each attorney's door and the level of care some people require. Attorneys are used to being "bothered." Remember, their skin is pretty thick.

Above and beyond all, trust that you're making the right decision. It's the right move in the direction you want to go, so even though you're afraid, you're going to be okay, it's going to be okay. It's this person's job to look out for you and, if you're anything like me, the idea of someone looking out for me, other than me, was a little foreign, but very comforting. And my attorney's words were music to my ears, "Just take care of your son. I'll take care of you."

That is just what I needed to hear. I was so tired, tired of arguing, tired of crying, tired of being confused, and just tired of being tired. I really needed someone to help me navigate the way forward, look out for pitfalls, and to protect my self-interest. In this situation, it was Sandra, and knowing that she had my back helped me sleep like a baby that night.

When creating my divorce plan, the thought of doing it myself didn't even enter my mind. I actually didn't know it was possible and thought not having an attorney wasn't an option. But, low and behold, in divorce, it seems everything is possible. And the DIY (Do It Yourself) divorce is definitely "a thing."

The first time I became aware of the DIY divorce was over coffee with my friend Cassie. When Cassie first met her husband Charlie, he was a breath of fresh air: fun, adventurous, and care-free—a wonderful reprieve from her obsessively responsible, over-achieving, by-the-book, people-pleasing self. They fell in love quickly and moved in together 3 months later. They were soon engaged. As she is telling me her story, she vividly remembers, after getting engaged, saying to Charlie "we shouldn't rush to set a wedding date." Afterall, things had already moved quickly, and she really didn't want to rush into marriage.

But, she was given an ultimatum—either get married or break up. It was as simple as that, and it was the start of a long ultimatum pattern in her marriage. Her gut told her this was not an okay ultimatum, but her brain said, "there isn't a 'real' reason to break up, so I guess we go ahead and get married." She went with her head, not so much her gut, and they were married, only one year and three months of total dating/knowing each other, for those of you keeping track.

"Manipulation and ultimatums—that's pretty much the gist of how I experienced marriage," she stated. "On the outside, we looked like the perfect and fun couple. But I was miserable, and I was behaving miserably. Not that there weren't any good times in the marriage—there definitely were some—but there were also many more not-so-great times."

It wasn't until seven years later that she knew she wanted a divorce. She recalls, "Charlie and I were sitting down on the couch, and he started to rub my feet. Nice huh? It wasn't often that things were done for me without some ulterior motive, but I was too tired to even think about what thing I'd be guilted into doing for a simple foot rub. I mentioned to him that it was nice to get a foot rub... and there it was, without skipping a beat, he responded, "Well, if we had kids then I'd do this more." Another F-ing ultimatum. You want me to do nice things? Then have kids. Her experience in marriage was just that. If she wanted something nice done for herself, she'd better be ready to go or give something in return. It wasn't about the idea or plan to have children. That was never discussed. "It was Charlie deciding what he wanted, and I better make it happen or else... I realized this relationship was either going to be more of me giving in and staying miserable or it was time for the marriage to end. At that moment, laying on the couch, I was exhausted with it all. I was done." Neither of them was happy. And both seemed to be doing their best. It's just that together, their "bests" weren't a good fit.

Wanting to be out of marriage was easy. Dealing with ending one was a bit more difficult. Cassie was determined to divorce on her terms, without legal counsel, as quickly and easily as possible. She was internet savvy, a millennial, and she knew that the more quickly she was able to complete her divorce, the sooner she would be able to begin her life. For her, freedom couldn't come soon enough. Their situation wasn't messy, there were no children, no assets, and very little debt. The decision to divorce was mutual, and they were both willing to be flexible on the terms. I recall her biggest complaint being the fact that she would have to wait 6 months for the divorce to finalize. That was it. Six months. Although many would feel like that wasn't much time, for her, that felt like a lifetime.

Although the DIY divorce can certainly speed up the process, I don't necessarily encourage it unless you also have legal counsel available to double check the facts. It's always advisable to have an attorney review the papers and represent you in court. Still, with do-it-yourself papers, you have the option to decide if you are comfortable doing them yourself, which reduces expenses. A DIY divorce is usually allowed only when the divorce is uncontested. An uncontested divorce is when two spouses have settled all major issues, such as child custody and spousal support. It sounds simple, but rarely is anything in life simple. Although many divorce may be uncontested, if you're anything like me, the idea of my soon-to-be-ex-spouse and I agreeing on EVERY major issue was a true fantasy. I mean, after all, we were divorcing for some very real life reasons.

But, if you're thinking a DIY divorce is for you, then the first step is to research what forms you need to file. Start with your state's website for forms. Many states provide these forms online and some states allow you to file an online divorce. If you cannot find the forms online, go to the county clerk's office or the divorce court clerk in person and ask for an uncontested divorce packet. Many states will have free packets at the courthouse. Also, note that divorce forms in many states are different for couples with and without children, so be sure to double check that you have the correct forms for your specific situation.

When it comes to a DIY divorce, essentially most of the work is left up to you. If you don't mind paying for an online service, one of the best sites available is Legalzoom.com. It is literally "one stop shopping" when it comes to legal information and forms. Legalzoom.com walks the reader through the process of finding and completing the necessary paperwork and setting one's divorce in motion.

The thing about divorce is that, regardless of who you hire, or if you manage the process yourself, it doesn't really ever go exactly as planned, and that's okay. What matters is you and what you need to do for you. Plans can change, so it's important to be flexible and remember that sometimes it's more about the journey than the destination. Divorce starts with one step, the first one, and doesn't have to be perfect, perfectly planned, or completely within your power or control. It just needs to happen.

CHAPTER 2

It's Like that Dream Where You're Naked

The decision to divorce is a deeply personal one, one that you understandably want to keep private. However, as much as you want, and have a right to privacy, there will inevitably come a point when you will need to share the news about your divorce with the other people in your life. Much of the process of sharing this news with friends, family, co-workers, and others involved in your life is considered on a "need to know" basis. Ask yourself this question, "Who needs to know what, and for what purpose?" It's also important to keep in mind that once that cat is out of the bag, information can take on a life of its own, so make sure the most important people in your life are informed first in order to prevent them hearing through the grapevine. First and foremost, take the advice of any celebrity who's had to deal with this and have a plan, a script if you will, and be prepared for a variety of responses and reactions.

If you have children, it's best if they are the first ones to hear about your decision. Whether your children are young or adults, they are the priority when it comes to disclosure. Possibly one of the hardest conversations you might have when it comes to sharing the news about your divorce will be with your kids, and the thought of it can feel overwhelming. However, this is one of the most critical conversations and one that needs thought and planning. The conversation that my soon-to-be-ex-spouse and I had with my son was, shockingly for me at the time, easier than I thought. He was nine years old at the time. We sat him down on the couch, told him that we both loved him, but that we couldn't be married to each other any longer. He asked us where we would live, cried for about a minute, and then asked if he could go hunt for Pokémon. I remember thinking, is that some kind of code for "I need a minute to process?" No, he was done with the conversation and had already moved on with his day. Truthfully, both of us were taken aback a bit by his response, but we took the break we got and sighed a bit of relief afterward. As a psychologist, I knew all too well that more questions would arise at a later date, so it was best to give my son the time and space he would need to allow him to process his thoughts and feelings. It was also important for him to know that if he didn't feel comfortable to talk to his dad or me about it, he could always seek out another adult in whom he trusted and felt safe to confide.

So where do you start with your own children? For starters, you must have a plan, and be sure to schedule a time to talk to your children on a day when there is enough time for questions to be asked and for feelings to be expressed.

Try to avoid having this conversation on a special occasion like Christmas or a birthday, one that might be tainted in the future as the day "mom and dad told us our family was being split in half." Although there are no perfect times, some are definitely worse than others. Although it is best not to avoid this conversation, pushing to have it too quickly can create more anxiety for all of those involved. It doesn't have to be bigger than it is and avoiding the conversation can create its own set of problems.

My client Tania first came to see me when she and her husband were deciding how and when to share the news of their divorce with their 9-year-old daughter. Although we discussed her plan in detail and set aside the right time and place for the conversation, this day came and went without any discussion being had. When I asked her why, she stated, "We don't really see the rush and we'd rather tell everyone at once." "What do you mean, exactly?" I asked. She stated that she didn't want friends and family finding out at different times, so they decided to have separate conversations with all parties, on the same day. I asked her directly why she felt the need to avoid having the conversation with her daughter. She seemed surprised by the question as she didn't have the sense she was avoiding talking to her daughter. I explained that we had originally agreed that it was more important for her to tell her daughter before telling anyone else, especially if there was a risk of her finding out after others, or even worse, through others. This was Tania's original plan, and it seemed valid and sound when we had discussed it two weeks prior. Nothing had really changed, other than Tania's fear and anxiety about the "unknown conversation." Putting it off felt more comfortable, and avoiding it all together at least in that moment, provided her with a little relief. Upon discussing it further, it didn't take long for Tania to realize that the longer she waited, the more anxious she became, and her daughter would definitely be aware of her mother's angst. Given this potentially emotional conversation, it is best to enter into it with courage and a calm head. Plus, avoidance quickly escalates a situation, and makes it bigger than it needs to be. Reminding herself that she would be okay, that her daughter would be okay, and open and direct communication, even with a 9-year-old, is truly the best way to tackle any serious conversation. Moreover, her daughter had felt, at least to some degree, the tension in her parent's relationship so she was not oblivious to the discord. Tania's daughter

was the most important person in her life, and when it came down
to it, she wanted to talk to her daughter about the future of their
family so that they could begin healing. It was the right thing to do,
and once she pushed past her fear, she was once again able to find
her voice.

If you and your soon-to-be-ex-spouse can do this together, it's
far better to share the news of your split with both of you present.
Sharing the news together is laden with many logistical and emotional benefits. It sets a positive tone for any co-parenting that
may need to occur, allows for consistency of shared information,
and gives your children the opportunity to ask questions of both
of you. It also reassures children that just because you are divorcing, doesn't mean that you can't be civil, or that they have to
choose a side. In Tania's situation, she was to be having this conversation without her husband present. He preferred to talk to his
daughter separately, and although this is not ideal, the alternative
was likely to create more emotional stress. When evaluating your
situation, take into consideration your ability to have a conversation with your soon-to-be-ex-spouse regarding your children. Be
honest about your emotions and how they can or can't be tem-
pered when having conversations directly with your children. In
situations where partners are not on speaking terms, the only option you have is to handle the conversation in the manner you
deem appropriate. You cannot control, nor do you have any say
in, how your partner will share this news with your children, so
rely on yourself to handle it in a way you see fit, and that is in the
best interests of your children.

If having this conversation together, it's important to remember that this is not your opportunity to debate the reason for your
divorce, it is your chance to handle an emotionally charged situation in a manner that protects and shields your children. It is critical that both of you refrain from accusing one another of any

wrongdoing and remain civil during this conversation. This conversation is solely to provide information to your kids in the healthiest way possible. The better behaved you are with each other in front of your children, the more likely they are to respect the two of you as individuals.

I can't stress this enough, try to have the conversation in person. Knowing that this may not always be possible, try to at least meet face to face. If you have adult children who live far away which deems a meeting in person, impossible, schedule a video chat. I know it might sound easier to handle this via text or email, but I can tell you the more impersonal the mode of communication, the higher likelihood of resentment. No one wants to open their email or message screen and be greeted with "Mom and dad are breaking up." I've seen it in my office, with my clients over the years, and the more damage you can prevent in the long run, the better. Once again, avoiding a conversation that should be face to face, although seeming easier in the short term, is likely to lead to hurt feelings, and possible estrangement.

If your kids have siblings, tell them all together. Even if they are different ages, from young child to adult, it's important that all children are told together in order to have the benefit of mutual support. Doing so also allows questions to be addressed right away, with all present, preventing the need to repeat things at a later date, or for information to become misconstrued when shared between siblings.

There's no need to go into that much detail, even if your children ask. Keep it simple and age appropriate. For younger children there are many age-appropriate books available to assist parents in communicating with their kids about their divorce. Telling your adult child may warrant a little more background or detail but try to refrain from oversharing. Remember, they are still your children, no matter how old, and telling too much can easily backfire.

However, be prepared for questions as to how this will impact them. Questions about extended family holidays, payment of college, etc., are commonly asked, and often the easiest of questions in which to respond. Older kids often have mixed emotions as to timing. Why now, 20 years later, why not back then? Answer these questions to the best of your ability, but still keep it simple. You don't need to know all of the answers. It's possible that your child isn't looking for answers and they know you can't really answer every question. Often, the stream of questions is more about frustration and confusion, and the "why's" are merely, "I don't understand but I know no answer will really change what's happening." Sometimes the best response is "I know this is a shock, and I wish I could answer all of your questions. But even if I can't, please know that I'm here for you and this divorce doesn't change my love for you in the least."

We all crave structure and security, and whether young or old, when decisions are made that directly affect us, we often feel powerless. Since knowledge is power, empower them with information that will directly affect their daily lives. Let them know what will be changing and what will be staying the same. Tell them you will do your best to keep them included when making schedule adjustments that directly affect them, whenever possible.

Explain who will be living where. For example, which parent will be staying in the house and which parent will be moving. For children still living at home, this information is directly relevant to their daily lives and lets them know how their living situation will differ from the present. Let your adult children know that although you will be living apart, that both of your homes are open to them and their relationship with you doesn't need to change because of your divorce.

Remind them that you love them and emphasize that none of this is their fault. This is critical, especially with younger children, in order to prevent unwanted anxiety and possible childhood trauma. Adult children often blame themselves as well, and wonder "what could I have done growing up to prevent this?"

Be prepared for a variety of feelings to be expressed. Children are unpredictable and often surprise us with either displaying no emotion at all, or by having a complete breakdown. Feelings can range from shock to relief, depending on the situation. Make sure you validate any feelings they choose to express. Your adult children are entitled to their own feelings, and they don't necessarily have to be happy for you; they might even feel anger. Give them the space to adjust to the news and to feel their emotions.

Keep an open dialog outside of this meeting so your children are free to process everything you've told them and ask any questions at a later date. This type of news will likely need some time to sink in, so don't expect every question to be asked and answered in one sitting.

After sharing the news with your kids, the next step is to take an inventory of who else needs to know, on a need-to-know basis. This is the stage in which essentially, your private divorce begins to go public. Similar to sharing the news of your divorce with your children, sharing with friends and family also requires having some kind of script in place. It's important to decide how much you want to share and hold true to your boundaries.

Since my family is quite small, telling the remainder of my family was fairly quick. They had been included during the process of my "decision", so telling them after I actually filed wasn't necessarily shocking. But that isn't always the case with everyone's family.

Truthfully, reactions may vary within a family. When I told my mom, "Simon and I don't hate each other. But we do both agree that being married is not only unhealthy for us, but especially toxic for our son," she didn't necessarily take the news "hard" per se, but I could tell that she was deeply affected. She knew it was the right decision, but it was tough for her to hear. Parents tend to be sensitive to our emotions, connected to what we feel far more than others in our lives. Our parents want us to be happy, and divorce is wrought with pain. But ultimately, our decision to divorce is designed to give each of us a happier life and reminding our family of this tends to soften the news.

My aunt and uncles' responses were very different. When I shared the news rather directly with my uncle, it was not a shock to him as he had been privy to our problems at that time. But the first response out of his mouth was, "Don't get a mediator, get a lawyer. And whatever you do, listen to what she says and don't be dumb." Wow, that was not exactly the response I expected, but it was supportive and useful. He was my uncle and warm and fuzzy wasn't exactly his style. Thankfully I knew that going into the conversation. He would go on to be a wealth of information, while my mom would wipe any tears as they came.

So how do you tell your family members? If the message is just meant to share the news with no desire to have a major conversation, then the best way is Sstraight to the point.

"I understand that this may come as a surprise, but after a lot of soul searching, we/I have come to this decision. It isn't something I care to talk about in depth right now, but we can talk further at a later date as I am still processing it all myself."

Letting your loved ones know that you understand their feelings, while also holding on to your boundaries, is not only fair to them, but fair to you as well.

After disclosing the news of our divorce to my son and immediate family, my next uncomfortable thought was "how am I going to tell my friends?" I was still feeling embarrassed and didn't want to be one of those divorced people that everyone felt sorry for. Plus, I didn't know how my friends were going to handle it, if they would be uncomfortable or, God forbid, possibly judge me like I was judging myself. The thought of telling them was one I faced with dread.

For some reason, the thought of telling my friends felt more awkward than any conversation with my immediate family. I wasn't as concerned about the possible judgment of my family. But I felt embarrassed, even ashamed to tell my friends. Part of this was due to my self-isolation as my marital problems became more significant. Because of the layers of problems Simon and I were having, I had begun to be more guarded and shied away from sharing our problems with my friends. I suppose shame about our struggles as well as his addiction caused me to detach from those who cared about me the most. Given my detachment, I guessed my friends would be dumbfounded, totally taken off guard by the news, and I felt completely unprepared for their re-actions. I wondered if they would ask questions, want to know details, and what degree of information would be appropriate given our relationship.

How would my friends react? Well, it can be mixed, not every-one will have the same response, so again, be prepared. But, it's safe to say that you can expect a variety of responses, from sup-port, to surprise, and some may even congratulate you.

I clearly remember one beautiful San Diego summer day at the first kid's birthday party I went to as a separated woman. I was nervous, my ex and I had only been separated for a short time, and I wasn't really prepared, nor did I have the opportunity to really think through how to share the news of my very recent separation with my son's friends parents, technically my acquaintances, so no one really knew much about the daily "goings on" of my life of late.

"Where's Simon?" I heard it over and over. "Couldn't make it" I responded just as frequently. But this got old, and I quickly dis-covered that the embarrassing, uncomfortable truth was better than any fiction I could create. This was less than ideal, and not part of my original plan of disclosure, but I felt put on the spot.

"We've separated," I said. And then, silence, I mean jaw-dropping silence. They were shocked, and I was shocked they were shocked. They knew us, as well as they could given our convenient relationships, how could they be that surprised? But they were and I suppose I understood. We all live in a bubble, a bubble full of our own lives, our own problems, families, jobs, and just regular daily drama. We don't and didn't talk about marital problems. We just assumed everyone was happy, partly because everyone was quite adept at faking it at times. I explained briefly that all of this was still very new, and both Simon and I were on good terms so there was no need for them to feel compelled to choose sides.

They shared their condolences, which, looking back, feels like such a strange response to me. I mean, nobody died, so why the condolences? Why not "congratulations?" It baffled me. And then they asked why. I wasn't sure how to respond so I answered, "He has a chemical dependency problem." This seemed to resonate for a few of them. They began to share stories of friends and family members who had similar problems, which made them relatable. Although this was validating, it was a lot of information being shared at what was supposed to be a kid's birthday party. Although these were friends, the relationships weren't as close as I had with others. Plus, this was supposed to be a light-hearted event and I was beginning to feel a little more vulnerable, and a little more naked. Sigh. It was turning out to be a long day. After a while the news had sunk into the minds of my friends and we all seemed to gravitate back into our respective roles, and I went to find the Chardonnay.

In a perfect world, when it comes to sharing the news of your divorce with friends, you will do so on your own time and at your own pace. But as you can see in the example above, rarely is our world perfect. Ideally, we'd be prepared for any and all questions, but that's really impossible. Thankfully the questions I received were minimal, probably due to the shock value of the news.

Remember that you don't have to answer any questions you're not comfortable answering and it is okay to let people know that you are still processing yourself. Try to press upon them that you just really wanted to share the news with them because their relationship matters to you.

Avoid negative statements about your spouse and reassure those close to you that you have no intention of asking them to choose sides. Focus on the fact that the marriage itself was a problem, not necessarily your partner. If you are sharing with mutual friends, this isn't the time to share your marital laundry, especially the dirty parts. Verbally bashing your spouse to mutual friends will most likely, ultimately, push them away which is not what you want. He can say what he wants; you have no control over that. The higher road here is one that not only preserves your integrity but also the integrity of your friendship.

When it comes to telling co-workers, just like others in your life, decide ahead of time how much you'd like to share. What is the least amount of information needed to share in order to get your needs met? Keep in mind that you have boundaries, and it is okay to maintain them, without fear of losing your job. Although it may go without saying, it is important to ask your colleagues to please respect your confidentiality. You would be surprised how often employers let this information leak out inadvertently, even with the best intentions in mind.

Again, be prepared for questions. For example, when telling your boss, he or she might have concerns about your ability to focus and remain consistent at work. Doing your best to assuage these concerns is probably going to be in your best interest. It's also possible that your company has an EAP (Employee Assistance Program), which can provide free counseling. Discuss this with your boss or consult with your Human Resources department as this is definitely worth taking advantage of.

In relationships with co-workers, it is important to try to keep your personal and professional life separate as much as you can. But, because we spend so much time at work, these relationships often intertwine. Sometimes our co-workers can provide support for us as well. Check in with your intentions prior to sharing and be mindful of any pitfalls that might occur as a result of disclosing this news.

If you and your spouse work together, create a plan to tell co-workers either together or individually but at the same time. What we're trying to prevent here is the painted picture of "water cooler" conversations with you completely in the dark. Many couples do indeed work together, so the need to create a plan in this situation is paramount. When it comes to divorce, chances are the stories you share will vary quite significantly from your spouse. But if the two of you share a workplace, it is imperative that you make sure you are on the same page. People shouldn't ask for detailed information, but the reality is, even if they don't, information will leak out. Remember in this situation that you control the narrative, and you definitely want to. Get ahead of the gossip by preparing a script and stick to it. If you and your spouse are on speaking terms, try to agree together how you will answer questions, and how much specific information you will share. Check in with one another regularly regarding any "workplace talk" so you don't end up being "the last to know" when it comes to your reputation. If there is considerable tension between the two of you, or if you are no longer speaking, consider involving your Human Resources Department with respect to the appropriate protocol in assisting to reduce any conflict at work, possibly a change in departments or office locations. Spouses who are divorcing yet work together presents a more complicated situation that often requires the involvement of management in the handling of day-to-day responsibilities or projects.

If you have children, you might need to share information with teachers, coaches, Boy or Girl Scout troop leaders, possibly school faculty, or any other extra-curricular activity providers. Try to remember that less is more in situations like this. Only share what you need to make things smoother for both you and your family. Discussing your situation with school staff and sports staff can be important when you are concerned about the impact the divorce will have on your kids. It also could be relevant when it comes to parental rights and responsibility regarding your child. Will there be changes in who picks up and who drops off? Are both of you still custodians of your child? In addition to "parenting logistics" the primary purpose of sharing this information with them is that they are in a position to monitor the behavior of your child and recognize times when he or she may behave differently as a result of the change in their home-life. Although this may feel embarrassing, trust me, I've been there. Once you share this information for the right reason, your child's well-being, feelings of shame and guilt dissipate.

I separated from my spouse when my son was in third grade. At that point I knew all of his teachers as I had volunteered in all of his classes throughout elementary school. Being a psychologist, I was well aware of the negative effects divorce could have on the mental well-being of a child, and how certain behaviors could manifest within the classroom. I needed her to know that we had separated, and I also needed her to know that I was the only parent with permission to remove my son from school if need be. His dad was in a treatment facility, and was needing to work on himself, so I was the sole caregiver at that time. Fortunately, she was a smart and savvy woman, so it didn't take much information for her to "get it." She didn't ask any personal questions and didn't appear to want to know more than I was prepared to share. I also realized that she genuinely appreciated knowing the information as she cared about my son and sharing what was happening with her directly was not only helpful but respectful. She was grateful, and I was very much relieved.

It's important to keep in mind that sharing information about your divorce with those who directly care for your child isn't about you necessarily. The information is useful in order to provide better overall care for your child. If your child is having a bad day, or is emotional, it is extremely helpful for caregivers to have an idea of what is going on in his or her home life. Every day, caregivers are forced to make assumptions about children and their lives in order to provide adequate care. Knowing just a little bit more about what is going on in a child's life can provide better understanding and often empathy when it comes to their "out of home" activities.

The choice to share this very private information is not to be trivialized either. Be selective in who decides to provide information and ask for discretion in sharing with others. Private information should be protected and respected with the sole purpose of sharing it to provide better quality of care.

In all of the above cases, keep in mind that this is your personal news to share, and not for others to repeat, unless that is something you are okay with. If so, inform those with whom you are sharing, what it is okay to repeat and what is to be kept to themselves. Sometimes those around us, even those who love us, need this gentle reminder. You can't stop everyone from gossiping, but a friendly reminder about discretion can go a long way.

Gentle Reminders

Reassure loved ones that this is a choice that is in the best interest of both you and your spouse, as well as your family.

Remind those who support you that you may need time and space to process, and to allow you that time, even if it may be difficult to understand.

Maintain your boundaries at all costs and remember that it's not only okay, but critical that you have conversations about your divorce on your terms, when you feel comfortable, and at your own pace.

Don't be surprised if many people have an opinion and have no problem sharing that opinion. Human beings tend to love giving advice, even if it's unsolicited.

If someone provides unwanted feedback, have responses ready so that you aren't taken entirely off guard. Practice saying things like, "Thanks so much for your feedback, I'll keep that in "mind, or, "Yes, there are many things to consider and think about during this complicated time." As you can see, the responses are fairly generic and can be applied to almost any unwarranted advice or feedback.

Allow family and friends to be there to support you and let them know you want that support from them. This is one of the primary reasons you are sharing the news with them in the first place.

The idea behind having something so private, eventually becoming public may start off as a necessary evil. But if the sharing is on your terms, although you may feel naked, you'll also feel stronger. The power of a secret is eliminated once it is shared.

CHAPTER 3

Who's In and Who's Out?

There's been a few times in my life when I had to learn the hard truth that not all friendships are meant to last. Although nothing lasts forever, you don't usually think of "breaking up" in relation to a friendship. But it can happen, and it can hurt almost as much, sometimes more, than a split with an intimate partner.

Divorce, whether it's acrimonious or amicable, tends to be accompanied by a significant change in our friendships, and for many, relationships forged during marriage tend to fall by the wayside. We'd like to think we don't really need to figure out who gets "custody" of whom, but often that isn't reality. This isn't necessarily a bad thing. Throughout life, friendships dissipate for different reasons, and sometimes this loss, followed by a shift in our social circle, can be a good thing.

When I was married, the friends "we" made, I made. Although Thomas was an extrovert, he had no interest in making friends. So, I made friends, and he socialized with them. I don't think that's unusual in marriages, and since I'm pretty extroverted myself, I was okay with it, at least until I got divorced.

When we separated, I assumed my/our female friends would remain loyal to me and if push came to shove, would lean in my direction to emotionally support me during my divorce. Don't get me wrong, my divorce wasn't a war by any means, and we do have a child so I understand the need for civility, but I did assume my good friends, and I mean GOOD female friends, would have my back. Well, I think we all know what happens when you assume; it makes an ass out of you and me.

I remember the day clearly. My son came home from school, plopped down on the barstool, and promptly said "Paula made me pancakes at daddy's house this morning." Now Paula, at this point at least, was a very close female friend of mine, and she was MY friend to be clear. Yes, she was a mutual friend, but as far as custody of friends, I assumed she was tethered to me. As I listened to my son prattle on about the fantastic breakfast Paula made for him, in Thomas's one bedroom apartment, I could feel myself become flushed. "She spent the night?" I thought. Why? How could that be? What were the kids doing? I mean she has two kids as well so what was the situation, and why? My head was reeling, and my poker face was waning. I needed to pull it together, for my son's sake.

I calmed my racing mind down and took a deep breath. I asked him where he slept, where everyone slept, because for starters, technically we were still married and our kids were present, and at best, this was extremely awkward. Apparently, this was a giant sleepover, and one that occurred quite frequently. I was stunned, confused, and then worried. I wasn't overly concerned about the two of them having an intimate relationship, they really weren't each other's type. My best guess was that drinking was involved which would warrant no driving. This thought wasn't exactly reassuring and the visual of them spending the night with one another, with all of our kids there, making breakfast in the morning, like one big, happy family, made my head hurt.

This wasn't good and felt like a betrayal. Women confide in female friends, we provide a listening ear, we keep each other's secrets, and have a "girl code," that creates this special bond which we count on to be a strong part of our emotional support system.

As I felt the walls slowly closing in, I sought out external support from my closest friends. Thankfully they also shared my disapproval and validated all of the many feelings I expressed. Although that helped considerably, I knew I still needed to have a conversation with Paula. Ugh, this was going to be awkward. So, of course, I sent her a text message. I didn't say I was brave, I was mad, but still nervous and feeling a little vulnerable.

When I asked Paula about the "sleepover," she appeared surprisingly nonchalant. "Yeah, we spent the night. It's no big deal really, I mean we're friends just like you and I are friends." I was shocked. How could she not get it?

So, I tried to explain my feelings simply: "Paula, I know you and Thomas spend a lot of time together doing things with the kids, and I'm able to make peace with it because I really don't want the kids lives to be impacted that much by the divorce so whatever can keep the status quo is ok with me, to an extent. But spending the night isn't the status quo, this is something new, and not only does it look bad, it also feels just wrong."

I thought I sounded pretty reasonable, understanding yet clear about my comfort level and boundaries. On the one hand, technically Thomas and I were still married, and on the other hand we were also in the process of going through a divorce and essentially suing each other, in the eyes of the law at least. Boundaries were, and are, critical for every party involved. Here's the interesting thing about boundaries: not everyone may agree to the terms, and individuals may not honor or respect them, which is why they are so critical. If others respected boundaries in the first place, we wouldn't really need to have conversations about them. But we do, often, throughout our lives.

Apparently, Paula didn't agree. She stated that she could be friends with both of us equally, in whatever manner she saw fit, and that I needed to accept that. I understood that and agreed that I had no control over her choices or how she should live her life, she was my friend and I couldn't understand how she didn't see that what she was doing was not only inappropriate, but extremely hurtful to me. Based on that, although I didn't have a say over her friendship with Simon, I did have a say when it came to her belief that she could stay friends with me. Clearly, my view of our friendship was very different from hers and I just didn't have the time or energy to salvage something with someone who I couldn't trust. I also realized that I had shared many more intimate details about pending court orders than I had initially thought, and I was quite sure my attorney would not want that information disclosed. I asked her kindly to keep everything I had shared with her about my thoughts, feelings, and plans about my divorce to herself. She said she was surprised that I could imagine her disclosing anything to my soon to be ex-husband. Really? She was shocked that I would think that about her. That was almost too funny. She agreed though, and I ended our dialog less-than satisfied.

After obsessing about this whole situation far longer than I had wanted, I resolved to chalk it up to a lesson learned. What my "friend" didn't realize apparently, was that by her taking her stance with my soon to be ex-husband under the guise of remaining both of our friends, and ignoring any boundaries, she was helping to polarize Thomas and myself and set us up for more conflict. I didn't expect her to discard my husband's friendship at the time, but I also didn't expect to be blindsided by her lack of respect for my boundaries, especially someone I considered a friend.

Friends are funny things. Some friends know what to do to show love and support. They break out the wine and know just what to say. They show up with a movie and a pizza just when you need a break, or plan a girls' night and encourage us to get out and enjoy life. And some friends disappoint us. My hunch is that Paula wasn't as good of a friend as I thought, and her handling of this situation, and disregard of my feelings, made that evident. But it did make me wonder how many other friendships, genuine female relationships of mine might change based on my status shift from being married to divorced, and whether or not that is a common experience for women who are divorcing. What I discovered is that this shift or loss of friendships is more common than not. The research itself is dated, but there's no denying the frequency of this morphosis.

In speaking with many women over the years, and despite vast differences in situations, one of the most recurring reasons for otherwise good friendships failing in the wake of divorce is fear; fear of change, fear of feelings; fear of the unknown. Yes, there are other reasons, but fear comes up over and over again.

People, including our nearest and dearest friends, often prefer the status quo; it's comfortable, familiar, and feels safe. We typically don't like change, or at least change that isn't within our locus of control. Nor do we like to grieve, and consequently, don't handle it well. We run from grief, ignore it, and avoid it whenever possible. It's the leading reason for referrals into therapy. The inability to manage negative feelings, which eventually ends up throwing us for a loop later on down the road. These feelings pass, but this fact doesn't stop us from trying to evade them in the first place. Divorce involves many feelings, including grief, not just for the couple, but for those close to them as well. And when the people we love hurt, we hurt as well. It's called empathy. Rarely do we "enjoy" feeling negative emotions, and when they sneak up on us, we usually do prefer them to be fleeting, or at the very least, like to be able to control them.

We want our friends to talk about their feelings, to be open and honest, vulnerable, and genuine. The foundation for human attachment is based on this authenticity. And, as women, we listen to each other share, cry, grieve, share some more, and so on. But, eventually, the negative feelings, frustration, confusion, anger, sadness can feel like too much and we prefer positive emotions, light-hearted stories, big smiles, and laughter. If levity isn't forthcoming, or is too infrequent, we create distance, pull away. It's often unintentional, but it hurts the receiver, nonetheless.

Divorce changes the status quo, and literally splits relationships right down the middle. The norm might have included intact families all sitting together at kids' soccer games, school events, etc. Divorce quickly changes that structure and creates a new normal. Often divorced couples sit on opposite sides of the park, or on the bleachers far away from each other, and that leaves many friends stuck in the middle and unsure as to what to do. What was "normal" and "comfortable" is now different, and change is inevitable. It's important to recognize that in most divorces, friends do choose a side, maybe not right away, but eventually they align with one spouse over the other. Although this may lead to polarization, it isn't uncommon when it comes to divorce, and hopefully it's done in a manner that's respectful, and again, honors one's boundaries.

As strange as it may sound, for some, divorce feels contagious. You might be surprised to find that if a friends' marriage is unstable or rocky, she might be more inclined to pull away from you for fear that her marriage will end up like yours. Shockingly, there is even research that supports this bizarre phenomenon.

A research team headed by Rose McDermott of Brown University analyzed three decades of data on marriage, divorce, and remarriage collected from thousands of residents of Framingham, Massachusetts. McDermott and her colleagues found that study participants were 75 % more likely to become divorced if a friend is divorced and 33 % more likely to end their marriage if a friend of a friend is divorced. "The contagion of divorce can spread through a social network like a rumor, affecting friends up to two degrees removed." According to Sociologists, the phenomenon is called "social contagion, and is the spread of information, attitudes and behaviors through friends, families, and other social networks. But, these findings are limited in that the study was conducted in the small town of Farmington where most residents either knew each other, were related to one another, or both. All were white, middle-class, employed individuals. The study is not an accurate representation of the country, much less a global one. But, it does make one curious as to how those staggering numbers are generated, and the impact on varying social relationships. McDermott, R. (2013) *Breaking up is hard to do unless everyone else is doing it. Social network effects on divorce, a longitudinal study. Social Forces.* 92 (2) pp. 491–519. https://doi.org/10.1093/sf/sot096.

Could the ending of one's marriage give others permission to examine their own marriage and its deficits? That thought was familiar to me. Is it that we often do have a "grass is greener on the other side" mentality? Regardless, the idea that divorce could be contagious, like the flu, could sound horrifying if you let it get to your head.

Sometimes, friends pull away due to the stigma that still exists about divorce. Divorce may be viewed as a failed marriage, a broken family, something of which to be ashamed thereby brandishing a giant scarlet letter across your chest. The idea of social contagion in which one's divorce may affect others like a virus, can be enough to spook a friend who is struggling in a tenuous marriage.

Many people also perceive married couples as mainstream and acceptable, and divorced people as part of a different culture, with more relaxed standards or morals. One study of young adults found that women who had been divorced more than once were viewed as being immoral or deviant. Hoffman, C. D., & Willers, M. D. (1996). *The effects of multiple divorces on person perception.* Journal of Divorce & Remarriage, 25, pp. 87-93.

Due to your new eligibility, you might be considered a threat now that you're single. When you were married, you were part of a couple, off limits, non-threatening. But that changes with divorce, and along with your new-found eligibility sometimes comes a perceived threat to the relationships of others. The thought, "Just because she doesn't have her own partner doesn't mean I'm going to let her take mine," has been referred to as "partner poaching." It may seem juvenile, and one would agree, but it happens more often than you'd think. I remember a colleague of mine telling me upon hearing about my divorce, "Remind me to tell you how differently you'll be treated by your married friends when you're the single woman in the group." And boy was she right.

I remember the first friend's birthday party I attended as an officially separated woman. All of our jointly-shared friends were there, and although I was anxious, I was relieved that the cat was finally out of the bag regarding my divorce, and was excited to see everyone. I chatted with friends, caught myself up on all the neighborhood gossip, and settled into the feeling that this was going to be just fine. It was then that Jonathan, the husband of my girlfriend Maggie, approached me. We hugged, as that's what we all do, and jointly chimed, "It's so good to see you!" And it was true, it was lovely to see everyone. We were both gobbling up birthday cake, when Jonathan commented, "Those glasses look great on you." It seems like an innocent comment, but not when the glasses were nestled in my cleavage. "Seriously," I thought. "Did he just really say that, or am I reading into something?" Feeling flushed, and beyond uncomfortable, I wasn't sure how to respond. "I mean, I'm just saying," he continued, probably recognizing the awkwardness as I hadn't yet responded. I calmly took a breath, and politely excused myself. To be honest, for a moment I thought of leaving. I felt embarrassed, like I had done something wrong. Logically, I knew I hadn't. But my feelings didn't match any logic. Maggie was my friend and her husband, essentially, had just made a pseudo-pass at me. Ewwww! His comment was disgusting, and he completely disgusted me. My idea of living quickly passed as I realized there was no way in hell I was going to let this asshole ruin my first free "playdate" with my friends. Thankfully I was able to successfully avoid him for the rest of the party, and thoroughly enjoy myself without giving him another thought.

Truthfully, I wish I could say that that was the only time something like that occurred. The reality is that that isn't the case. I've had friends' husbands make lewd comments, smack my butt, and one even bit my neck. Yes, it was gross, and he is a pig. And I know, in my oh-so-reliable gut, that if my ex-husband had been with me at the time, there is no way any of them would have ever acted so inappropriately. The fact that I was now single, for some reason in their minds, gave them permission to cross so far over a boundary, there would be no going back. Those female friends remained my friends, but I made a very conscious effort to steer clear of their "sexually-harassing" partners.

One of the most valuable assets that you can have, especially during your divorce, is a caring friend, a friend who reserves judgment and criticism. A good friend, a reliable friend, a "keeper" is one who will not leave you in direst of times, regardless of their reservations. It's critical to recognize and appreciate the friends we have that share our values, who can relate and empathize, and be there for us, especially during the difficult times. As Oprah Winfrey once said, "Everyone wants to ride with you in the limo, but what you want is someone who will take the bus with you when the limo breaks down."

But friendships do take work, on both sides. This is especially important to be mindful of when going through a divorce and wanting to hold on to those friends worth holding on to. If keeping mutual friends is of importance to you, take the initiative to talk to those friends and reassure them that you won't ask them to take sides. Let them know you recognize that this is a difficult situation, but ultimately divorce isn't about devastating relationships, it's about making the lives of all people involved happier and more fulfilled.

Venting to a trusted confidant can facilitate healing, but your venting might be a little too much for your friend to handle at times, especially if this is a mutual friend of both you and your spouse. Remember that as much as you have emotional needs, your friend does as well, so be mindful of your boundaries and be respectful of his or hers as well. You might be surprised that the friends who do stick around, become better friends and your relationships with them may become stronger. I noticed this over the years immediately following my divorce. Most of our "couple" friends drifted away, but a few of the friendships I made during our marriage, not only remained intact, but flourished into lifelong relationships. As I changed, they changed, and definitely for the better.

You also may notice that due to your divorce, you actually have more time for friends. I recognized that much of my time during the last two years of my marriage was devoted to trying to save something unsavable and this fruitless task can be extremely time consuming. My friends had missed me, and I missed them. Many women have a tendency to push friends aside to prioritize their spouse, which is understandable, but close friends are too important to be ignored. Our emotional and mental strength comes, in part, from the strong bonds we have with each other, and recent research shows that the average female relationship lasts 16 years, which is 6 years longer than the average romantic relationship. Since women are a significant part of each other's emotional support systems, strong and healthy female relationships can be of benefit to all women.

The beauty of divorce is that it allows you to grow into your own person, with your own life, and your own needs. You are responsible for you right now, not your marriage or your spouse, YOU. Change can be scary, and it can be exciting, but the one thing it most definitely is, is constant. Change is a gift that affords us the opportunity to adapt to new environments, new situations, and new people.

Divorce involves a great deal of change, on many levels, which gives us an opportunity to learn and grow. Friendships are a part of that reformation, and as we change, they will as well. So much of ourselves gets ignored, silenced, brushed aside when we try to make a marriage work that, for whatever reason, isn't meant to. By suppressing who you really are in marriage, going along in order to get along, your own feelings are ignored and the real you tends to get minimized or even forgotten at times. When you no longer have to fight to keep these feelings down, to defend yourself, you are free to be your authentic self. It is when you experience your authentic self that your self-esteem naturally grows, leading to a healthy and happier you. The best version of you. Your divorce, a significant change in your life, provides you with the opportunity to forge new relationships, stronger and valuable connections based on who you are as a person, as an individual, and as a woman who deserves the same emotional support you give to others.

As a therapist working with individuals for more than two decades, I've learned that although people want to connect with one another, we can become a little intimidated by the idea. Wanting someone to be your friend also requires you to make an effort, to seek people out, and actively be a good friend to that person. And making friends when you're older, is no easy feat. We're busy with our careers, our kids, our extended families, and just our often over-packed, busting-at-the-seams, everyday lives. Yet we are social beings. Biologically, we are wired to attach to others. So how do you break out of your comfort zone and start finding new friends? Is it as simple as standing in a line at your local market, seeing another person who looks like "friend material" and jumping in with, "Wanna be friends?" Well, as silly as that might sound, yes, it can be that simple.

When I divorced and my ex-husband was able to have my son two days out of the week, I found myself with even more free time. At first this felt very strange, and honestly, a little lonely. I contacted a friend from a Pilates class and asked what her plans were. She was working her night job as a bartender at a local wine bar. I thought, "I like wine, maybe I could go and just sit and chat with her." And that's exactly what I did. I went by myself, put my big girl pants on and ventured out solo, to that unknown world of singlehood. Here's the thing, it wasn't as scary as I thought, and it was actually really fun. Plus, I wasn't the only person there by herself. Who would have thought that many, many single people, like me, enjoy meeting new people. That night I met two new female friends who quickly became better friends, and those friendships have grown into ones I value dearly.

Take a chance and try to cast a wide net by being open to getting to know someone you hadn't really thought of as a potential friend until now. If you work, scan your workplace for "like minds" and become a little more friendly with a potentially new friend. If you aren't employed, then think of volunteering somewhere, anywhere. Volunteering doesn't take a major commitment and typically non-profit organizations are just grateful for your time. Volunteering is a great way to connect with others who share similar values, and appreciation for the "cause." What better way to connect with someone than doing something for the greater good. As a side benefit, helping others, also known as "random acts of kindness," is one of the most effective forms of staving off depression.

If you have children, reach out to other parents, even if it's just to say "hi" and become more familiar with who your children are spending time with. Set up a playdate with one of your kid's pals and make sure to tag along, even if it's for a little while. Or, better yet, invite the family over to your place for a casual "meet and greet."

When my son started kindergarten, I remember feeling so completely overwhelmed with trying to keep track of everything I needed to do for his 3-hour day. I recall thinking that kindergarten would provide me with a bit of a break, but instead it bumped up my to-do list to another level. Thankfully, included in our kindergarten packets was a phone roster of parents. This list of contacts allowed me to reach out and to set up a mom-pool of combined efforts, a very special godsend for us working moms with plates overflowing. Some of these women are still my dearest and most treasured friends. We understand each other, accept one another, and often tease each other as we reflect on life's mishaps.

Meetup.com is a great resource to meet people. It was created after September 11 as a way for people to provide support to one another and now it is a massive resource for its subscribers to explore activities, clubs, and special interest groups as a means of improving their quality of life and to connect with others. From dog walkers, to hikers, to movie-goers or wine tasters, it provides an abundance of seemingly limitless options for people to meet and get to know one another while sharing mutually appreciated activities. It's free, and designed for the "solo" participant, by a solo participant who started their "meet up" as a means to meet others. Don't be afraid to attend alone; that's its purpose, to connect people.

Although life is full of endings and new beginnings, hellos and goodbyes, losing a good friend, especially during your time of need, hurts more than just a little. As I felt those feelings and thought of all of the reasons why this happens, I became even more resolved in sharing my story about Paula, to help other women going through the trials and triumphs of a divorce. I don't know Paula's motives for making the choices she made in our friendship, especially since she too was a single mom, trying to do the best that she could in a society crippled by judgment and criticism. But I reminded myself that the choices other people make for themselves, although uncomfortable in the moment, may end up benefiting us in the end. This acceptance was reinforced when I realized the importance of nurturing my "all weather" friendships, and recognized and appreciated the newly blossoming buds of new found friends as well.

CHAPTER 4

It's Not all Rainbows and Unicorns, But it Will Be Okay

Whew! You're done! You've checked all of the "to do" boxes on your attorney's lengthy list and, for all intents and purposes, should be officially divorced, right? Well, not in California, or in most states for that matter. In California, the state requires you to file your paperwork and wait exactly 6 months, affectionately called the Cooling Off Period. The Cooling Off Period is designed to allow the two of you to take enough time to fully decide that you truly want to become divorced. This 6-month period feels like a lifetime. I remember waiting, and waiting, and thinking, "Why does everything in life seem to happen so quickly, except for divorce?" The process seems to go on forever, or at least it feels like that at the time. But, wait you must.

I think, as most of us who have ever had to experience something traumatic, once the dust settles, it is then that the feelings tend to kick in. And sometimes the kick is a little stronger than we imagine. Going through my divorce seemed akin to planning my wedding. There were periods of time that I was needing to fire from all cylinders to get in paperwork, etc., and other times I had to just sit back and wait, and wait, and wait.

Making the decision to divorce is more than an intellectual one; it's one that comes from the heart as well. And just as you went through the process of dating, courting, getting to know one another, etc., the process of divorce also requires many steps. As much as your brain is required to think clearly during this process, more often than not, a multitude of emotions will prevail.

Where are they coming from? How do you deal with them? When will they pass? And what do they mean? These are all questions that may be running through your mind.

I remember one client sharing her experience by saying, "At first, I was elated, 'over the moon relieved' that my ex-spouse was gone. And then, a few weeks later, I was intensely sad. The sadness took me off guard as I was the one who initiated our divorce. It just didn't make sense. Or maybe it did, I just didn't understand what I was feeling and why."

What are the feelings we're "supposed" to feel when going through a divorce? Truthfully, they can be all over the board, without rhyme or reason, and on no particular schedule. You may feel conflicting emotions, anger one minute, fear another, and then relief. Thankfully, all of them will pass, eventually. I recall reading in numerous articles that there are 7 feelings that occur during divorce, much like the stages of grief. Only 7 feelings, really? I'm pretty sure I counted more feelings on all my fingers and toes, and that was in one day.

Feelings of grief, sadness, and loss can be related to many aspects of your marriage. Loss of perhaps your children, of your house or financial security, or even the overall loss of what once was. The feeling of loss is inevitable. I remember not quite feeling loss over my ex-husband, but a sense of loss over losing my in-laws. I loved my mother-in-law; we had a closer relationship than I had with my own mother. I could always count on her to be there for me, as I was there for her. We talked all of the time, shared our pins on Pinterest, and texted random memes to each other constantly. We were pals.

When I filed for divorce, I never dreamed that I wouldn't hear from her again. I tried calling and texting, multiple times, but I heard nothing back. I even sent birthday cards and Mothers' Day flowers, but I still didn't hear anything from her. Eventually reality sunk in, and I realized I was being ghosted by my mother-in-law. For whatever reason I went from hearing "Please, call me mom" to "don't ever call me again." I knew many other divorced women who remained close with their in-laws, but this wasn't the case in my situation. I couldn't figure out what I had done wrong. I was confused, disappointed, and heartbroken. I felt abandoned, and it hurt, a lot, for far longer than I thought a feeling should. But eventually it passed, and I came to accept the reality, even without fully understanding why she did what she did. Acceptance of a painful situation allows us the freedom to let go.

The sadness you feel might be related to the loss of your ex-husband himself. Perhaps he was the one who made the decision to divorce, and it's not what you wanted. Or maybe it was a mutual decision, but you still feel sad about letting him go. The reality is it is hard to let go of someone you love. Perhaps you miss him, miss what you once had, and those memories are stuck in your head, just replaying over and over again. We call this nostalgia. When we feel nostalgic, we tend to look through "rose-colored glasses," and we forget the gray, the bad, the ugly memories. So, our memories are skewed. Because of these rose-colored glasses we are unable to recall the bad times, the painful moments, the moments that lead to the divorce in the first place.

We all have good memories, and we all have painful ones as well. Take a moment to rebalance your memories. Start writing down all of the "negative traits" about your ex. Initially you may not be able to recall them, but, believe me, once you get started, you will probably discover that the list is quite long. If you feel like you will never find someone else like him, remember the saying, "If you can love the wrong person so strongly, imagine how it feels to love the right person."

If you are still in contact with your ex-spouse, whether you have children or you don't, really examine the reasons for the contact. If there are still "feelings" between the two of you, any contact is going to make getting over him exponentially difficult. Often people, myself included, will manufacture an excuse to make contact with an ex-partner. As rational as the reason for the "reach-out" might seem, often it is merely a cloaked excuse. I've witnessed within the four walls of my office, on more than once occasion, clients saying things like, "Well, I had to reach out to Joe because he needed to talk about our son's dental cleaning that's coming up in three months." Hmmm, is that really necessary? Honestly, when I got divorced, I really had no desire to talk to my ex-husband, even if I had to for some reason; in those situations, I quite frankly, dreaded it. But if you find yourself "wanting" to make contact, even if it feels like a valid reason, it probably is not in your heart's best interest to do. When it comes to break ups, there's something called the 30-day "no contact rule." The rule is, no contact for 30 days, for any reason. This time allows you the space to resist any urges, or impulses, and to ride the wave of your emotions, until they eventually subside. At the end of 30 days, you will be less likely to want to reach out as you will have a better chance to do some healing.

Perhaps you are in denial. Denial is a healthy, normal, and vital part of the grieving, but it does have its place. Denial is present to assist us in integrating painful situations and is the coping mechanism that helps us to avoid feeling a flood of intense emotions all at once; it helps us take things in, a little at a time. The problem with denial is that if it continues on longer than it should, it can be quite destructive. Typically, someone who is cocooned in denial is struggling with receiving the emotional support they need to work through the divorce process. Without that support, the comfort of denial feels like a womb that protects and shields us from the harshness of reality. Support can come from varying sources. Friends, family, therapist, life-coach, or a sense of purpose that is separate from that of being married.

Feelings of loneliness can creep in throughout the divorce process. It is bearable, but we, being social beings, truly dread and try to avoid feeling lonely at all costs. But it's important to remember that being alone and feeling lonely are two different things. Have you ever felt lonely but were in a relationship at the time? That can feel far worse. Feeling lonely while being alone is appropriate and congruent, and unpleasant as it is, tolerable. Therefore, feelings of loneliness at this time are unpleasant but a very normal and a necessary part of the process.

Two of the most uncomfortable feelings that one experiences are that of guilt and shame. Although guilt can feel more tolerable than shame, it can, more often than not, stop us dead in our tracks. If we have a conscience, then we are familiar with the feeling of guilt. It is often a healthy response in a specific given situation. However, that feeling alone doesn't always coincide with responsibility. A sense of guilt can allow us to reflect on behavior, determine the level of responsibility, and then make appropriate changes to avoid a negative outcome in the future. However, if left unattended, guilt can take over, become unhealthy and paralyzing, and lead to feeling so shame. If guilt is a young child, shame is its big brother.

Often the key to working through our feelings is assessing our thoughts. A feeling isn't something we have power or control over, it is just a feeling. But, if our thoughts and perceptions make our feelings more intense, then we owe it to ourselves to examine these thoughts in the moment. In therapy, we call this Thought Monitoring. We begin by noting our automatic thought that occurs either before a feeling, or right after. We then examine the evidence that either proves or disproves that feeling. For example, I might feel guilty because my marriage didn't work, and that feeling may feel so intense that I am angry with myself. Based on those feelings, it isn't a reach to say that I view myself as responsible for the marriage itself. But, this isn't necessarily the case. A relationship is based on two people, not just one. There were times the marriage did work, and then times that it didn't, so neither of us received all of the blame or credit. The responsibility is shared. Although that may not completely eliminate feelings of guilt, restructuring our irrational thought patterns can often help alleviate enough to make the feeling more tolerable.

When asked why all of her marriages had failed, anthropologist Margaret Mead is said to have replied "I beg your pardon; I have had three marriages and *none* of them was a failure." Unfortunately, although this may have been more common historically than at present, society still perceives divorce as quitting, of giving up, of not being strong enough to endure. All of these perceptions question one's worth and value, and stigmatize a person during divorce. Not wanting to be the kind of person who gets divorced is often the belief, as if there is a definitive "kind" in the first place. And god forbid you have children. Society is especially judgmental in shaming those with children by saying that they are failing to consider the needs of their kids. It is interesting that among highly educated Americans, about half of them think that divorce should be made more difficult. And only 17 % of educated Americans agreed with the statement "Marriage has not worked out for most people I know" compared to 58 % of less educated Americans." Kliff, S. (2016) *Americans think divorce is less acceptable than they did a decade ago.* Vox. https://www.vox.com/2016/3/17/11250888/divorce-public-opinion-united-states

Failing at something is a natural occurrence, a behavior. Our behaviors are what we do, they aren't what we are. When our thoughts are distorted and we are seeing things in black and white terms, all or nothing, and overgeneralizing, we are likely to see ourselves as actual failures. When we dispute these thoughts and restructure them based on the evidence, we realize that nothing is absolute, not even a marriage. Regardless of how long you were married, you were successful during those years. The marriage worked, until it didn't any longer. That is not a failure, not in the least.

Maybe you think you're just not good enough, should've recognized the problems sooner, stayed too long, or shouldn't have married the wrong person. All of those messages, each one contradicting the other, and lacking any foundation in reality, still add fuel to the fire of guilt and shame. Whether someone points a finger at you, or whether it's the voice of your own inner critic, the judgment can be thick, and the guilt based on perceived wrong choices can be relentless.

I know on many occasions during my divorce, I felt anger. It would come on fast, usually after I received some random text message from my ex that would send me off the rails. But it wasn't easy, not in the least. We all feel anger, whether we like to admit it or not.

I recall meeting Monica, who entered my office on the heels of a recent breakup. She was hurt, disappointed, confused, and very angry. Her fiancé had broken up with her on Christmas Eve. She had understandably had a right to feel all of her feelings, especially anger. We worked together initially on just helping her to get through her daily activities as she was completely traumatized. After a while, when she was more stable, yet still very angry, we began to explore more of the interpersonal dynamics of her relationship. It was then that I asked her what acceptance of responsibility she was able to take for the ending of their relationship. She was surprised by the question as she was clearly the victim in this tragedy. I didn't disagree. She was indeed victimized as her fiancé dropped a bombshell on her on Christmas Eve, without warning. But the question was still relevant, and highly appropriate. Every relationship involves two people, two consenting people who both get the credit and the blame for the successes or failures of a relationship. Was her fiancé a complete jerk for the way he handled this breakup? He most certainly was. Does anyone deserve to be disrespected in that manner, especially someone you are planning on marrying? No, everyone deserves respect. But, that doesn't mean that one person is to blame for the ending of a relationship. Plus, holding on to this belief not only keeps you stuck in anger and resentment, it also renders you helpless and powerless. It was not only important for Monica to explore her level of responsibility in the relationship in order to get past her anger, it was critical for her ultimate healing.

According to research done by Tashiro and Frazier, people experience relationship dissolution differently, depending on whether they initiated the breakup. "Research has demonstrated that non-initiation is linked with experiencing a breakup as more stressful and feeling less recovered, which they suggest is likely due to feeling a lesser amount of control over the breakup." So essentially, our feelings and sense of control are strongly correlated. How do we recover that control and that power in order to heal and recover more quickly? Tashiro, T. and Frazier, P. (2003), *"I'll never be in a relationship like that again": Personal growth following romantic relationship breakups.* Personal Relationships, 10: 113-128.

One of my favorite therapeutic techniques is Dialectical Behavior Therapy (DBT). The process of DBT begins with being mindful of one's feelings, then learning to tolerate distressing emotions, followed by the improvement of interpersonal relationships. The term dialectical refers to the practice of acting in an opposing behavior of an expressed emotion. So, if you're feeling anxious, then engage in a relaxing activity to reduce the negative feeling of stress. If you're feeling angry, the diffusion of that anger is the best course of action. But how does one act in a manner that opposes anger? Certainly, we have all experienced the words of a friend or partner telling us to calm down when we are angry, and we all know these words tend to do the opposite. After all, we feel what we feel, and merely instructional words aren't going to change that. But, the idea isn't too far off. In DBT, we instruct our clients who may be experiencing extreme anger toward another person to attempt to manage this distress by focusing on something they may appreciate or even admire about this person, rather than the ways in which they might feel wronged or taken advantage of.

Often, the acceptance of responsibility, followed by the act of practicing forgiveness is the first step in letting go of anger. For Monica, it was critical for her to begin to examine her role in the breakup, even if the percent is negligible, she still played a part. By doing so, she was able to shift some of her anger away from her ex-partner, thereby allowing herself to begin to accept all facets of her breakup.

Managing one's anger, as opposed to suppressing it, is one of the best tools available. Recognize that you probably have a right to feel angry, and that all emotions, even anger, are present for a reason. Anger presents itself when you feel threatened or under attack. It acts in unison with our body's natural fight or flight response and is responsible for the fight. Random moments of thought that send your emotions on a roller coaster ride are called triggers. These triggers are just like the trigger on a loaded gun. If there's no ammunition, then the trigger is useless. Intense emotions are typically the result of the combination of a triggering event, a person's individual characteristics, and their appraisal of a particular situation. In other words, if I am hurt, and my appraisal of the situation is one in which I interpret someone hurting me on purpose, my anger is quite likely to escalate. Although it is a very natural and normal emotion, and one necessary for our survival as a species, often it can tend to render someone out of control if it is not managed. And repressed anger, much like a steaming pot of water, not attended to can easily boil over into a disastrous mess.

If you find that you and your ex-husband engage in dialog that can be triggering, then as both a preventative measure, as well as an "in the moment intervention," try to avoid power struggles. As tempting as it may feel to engage in a mental or verbal tug of war, try to resist. It will only end up mentally exhausting you even more in the long run. Not every battle warrants a war, especially with someone who you know no longer has as a daily part of your life. He's not your husband anymore and there's nothing to prove. He just doesn't matter that much.

Fear is another common emotion I think all of us humans are familiar with. And fear during divorce can run rampant, across a variety of unknown situations, venturing into the unknown is scary, plain and simple. We don't like change, and we like it even less when it is out of our control. As you venture into a new life, a new future, you might be fearful. After all, you're going to be single again, and the world might look a little different from the last time you were in it and on your own. Understandably, you might feel anxious. Our partners help us in life, that's what makes them partners. Perhaps he was a great cook and you can't boil water, or maybe he was a financial whiz kid and, if you're like me, instead of QuickBooks you use a Nordstrom bag for your receipts. You might feel incapable of doing the things he did for you, the way he did.

Perhaps you're afraid of making the same mistakes again. When we experience trauma, as in divorce, we tend to get gun shy. After one relationship ends, the last thing we want is more heartbreak. I recall a long-ago conversation with my mother-in-law about her history with two ex-husbands. Both were bad, I mean really bad. One was an abusive alcoholic, which was my ex-husband's father, and the other was a complete narcissist. After the end of her second marriage, she decided to never date again. That was it for her. At 45 years of age, she resolved to remain celibate, and chalked it up to two bad choices being enough for one life.

Many feelings such as the ones we tend to experience when going through divorce are tolerable. But what happens when we experience feelings that are extremely distressing, and consequently intolerable? What do we do about them?

We humans are smart, sometimes a little too smart for our own good. Take the feeling of anxiety for a moment. We feel fear, as a result of the same flight or fight response that all animals experience, but because of our prefrontal cortex and our ability to use language, we are able to assess a situation and then act rather than just react accordingly. Our ability to think, and process as a result of our executive functioning, has allowed us to soar to the top of the food chain. But, along with our ability to think is our tendency to overthink, to over analyze, which gets many of us into trouble. Because we have language, we question, interpret and conclude as a means to understand and often control a situation. This pattern of overthinking leads to the creation of assumptions, sometimes with minimal information. An assumption is an unexamined belief and one in which we think without realizing we think it. If we jump to a conclusion about a feeling, and create an assumption, our feelings can become more intense, more powerful, and often feel intolerable.

This is what I call falling down the rabbit hole. The further down the hole you get, the harder it is to get out. And getting out is exhausting.

On the other hand, giving in to your anxiety makes the fear greater. For example, if I am worried that I will never find another partner in my life who will make me happy, I might give up and never put myself out there to meet someone again. This plan is designed to keep me safe, but it won't make me feel safe. The tinier I make my world because I am afraid to get hurt, the more fearful I become, and now, in addition to fear, I will likely also feel lonely, resentful, and bitter. That's not to say that being alone creates those negative feelings but doing so based on fear only strengthens it. By doing so I deprive myself the opportunity to see if the emotions I'm afraid of are tolerable. I also do not allow myself to discover my own strength, which increases the fear. If I'm too afraid to try, how will I ever know how bad, or even good, the experience could have been? Plus, positive experiences are the ones that help carry us through the negative ones. Without heartbreak, sadness, or disappointment, how else will we ever have hope?

Acceptance is the key to tolerating your emotions, not attaching too much meaning to them, and leaving them as they are, just feelings. When we create a "story" or a narrative as I call it, to our feelings, then often intensify. For example, I recall feeling intense fear when my ex-husband lost his job during the process of our divorce, and my mind raced in a thousand directions, all of them ending up in scenarios that were terrifying. As I pummeled down the rabbit hole, I remember thinking, "Oh my God, I'm going to have to pay alimony, or child support, and I won't see my son, and it will be just like the last 5 years of my marriage... and I'll be stuck!" Once I calmed down, I realized that this wasn't necessarily the case, that my ex merely had gotten laid off with a severance package, and even though I would need to spend a little more money on the divorce than I had anticipated, it really wasn't going to be as bad as I thought. It was still upsetting, and stressful, but the "narrative" I had created in my head was highly unlikely to happen. And that is the critical thing about anxiety, there are two rules. It will never be as bad as you think, and you will always overestimate danger.

How do we deal with emotions? How do we manage on a daily basis, without being at the mercy of our feelings?

The key is learning to manage your anxiety, rather than attempting to feed it, or suppress it. If you find that you can't push these intrusive thoughts out of your head, which is sometimes the case in anxiety, schedule time to obsess. This may sound crazy, but it works. Intrusive thoughts are just that, intrusive. They pop in and out of your head on their own terms and allowing them to take over can be mentally exhausting. Rather than fighting the thoughts all day long, allow yourself an hour each day, pre-arranged, to worry. And then force yourself to sit down during that time, whether you "feel" like it or not, and go through all of your thoughts one by one for that hour. At some point you will become bored, which is what you want.

Give yourself the opportunity to "feel your feelings" and let them just be. The truth is, the more you fight them the stronger they will fight back. Imagine yourself on one side of a tug of war rope, with your feelings holding the other end, and a giant hole in the middle. You may think that the harder you pull the stronger you will become and the less likely you will be to fall in that hole. But the reality is that you are fighting yourself, and the harder you fight the more likely you are to fall into that giant crevice. What would happen if you just let go of the rope? Just dropped it and gave up the fight? The feelings might not go away, but that is tolerable. Far more tolerable, and less exhausting than the battle you engaged in with yourself.

Recognize that you might not be operating at your highest level right now, and that's okay. You might not be as productive, focused, the life of the party, or motivated at all. Expect that this is part of the process and it will pass, just give yourself some time to heal. We are all typically much better at giving a physical wound time to heal, we are patient with that healing process and know that eventually our body will repair itself if we take care of it and give it time. But, for some reason, we aren't very patient or understanding of our emotions and we demand that they get better quickly so we can move on to bigger things.

Practice self-care. The combination of physical health and mental health care are both critical at this time. I know that we often talk about self-care as a given, but it's one of the first things to fall by the wayside when going through divorce. There's so much to be done, so very much, and just not enough hours in the day to do it. But, at this stage in your divorce, your "divorce to do list" is done, so take a breath. Identify the aspects of self-care that you might've been ignoring until now and make them a priority once again.

Start with the basics: Sleep, nutrition, and exercise. Make sure you're getting enough sleep. This is critical. Without enough sleep, our brains cannot function to their capacity and we become more easily agitated and frustrated. This is not something you can afford during this period of time, so make sleep a priority. Remember that what you put into your body is what you also get out of your body, so try to feed your body the way you would feed your child; make yourself a meal, pack a lunch, and don't skip breakfast. Try to stay active, at least as much as you can. Our bodies are designed to be mobile, with two arms and two legs. Physical activity at least three times per week helps stave off depression and regulates our emotions. During divorce, we often need more than just a little help with navigating our feelings.

Practice being mindful. The term "mindfulness" seems to be used now more than ever, and is just as vague and ambiguous in its definition. In my private practice, I stress the importance of learning to be mindful, during every session with my clients. But this process is easier said than done. Mindfulness is the self-regulation of attention with an attitude of curiosity, openness, and acceptance. There is no room for judgment or assumptions when being mindful. The purpose is to be objective, to be in the moment and to be present, which is the opposite of overthinking. Yoga, meditation, guided imagery, are all ways in which people practice being mindful on a daily basis. Journaling is one of the best mindful activities that I recommend. Try writing your thoughts down on paper. Don't worry about how it sounds or what it says, just recognize your thoughts and feelings and make note of them, without judgment. There are also many phone applications that teach one to be mindful through breathwork, or mindful activities to learn to be in the moment, aware of all of your senses, and to bring purpose to your activities.

Get the support that you need in your situation. Being a therapist, I cannot stress enough the importance of self-care and obtaining as much emotional support during this difficult time. I believe that all therapists should have their own therapist, and I have one on retainer, just in case I need her. During my divorce she earned that retainer, many times over. There are also divorce support groups available as either a part of many therapy group practices or through referral websites, such as Psychology Today or Therathrive. Your attorney or mediator might also have a referral to one, you merely need to ask.

The support from family and friends is so very important, but that support can only go so far. People have their own lives to live, and eventually listening to you share your thoughts and feelings might become a little tedious for them. The idea is that you want to maintain these relationships, not wear them thin. Seeking out a support group, or therapist, can assist in the healing process as you utilize this expertise to help you through all of the emotions you might have. This investment, whether it be time, money, or both, is an investment in you, and your future. Nothing is more valuable than that.

The Help and Hindrance of Social Media on Our Emotions

In today's society, more often than not, people turn to their social media platforms as a mode of informing and communicating every thoughts, usually, at the moment the thoughts occur, and often when they are the most vulnerable. This can be both positive and problematic when you are in the middle of a divorce, and examining the cost benefit analysis is worth your time. In erroring on the side of caution, I've always told my clients, "If you're feeling something over a "5" don't do anything. Allow your emotions time to settle down before simply reacting.

When Darlene came to see me, to say she was distressed is an understatement. Like many of us, she was a regular Facebook user with hundreds of online friends. She was in the midst of a divorce for the past six months and was utilizing her social media as a way to obtain validation and support from others. On that particular day, it backfired. She had posted on Facebook a story about her ex-husband and his new girlfriend. She had found pictures of them on their vacation and used this opportunity to disparage him for his excessive use of funds and his "bad taste" in women. Unfortunately, the feedback she received was not exactly what she expected. Although many Facebook friends supported her, there were also many who suggested she stay out of his life as it was not her business. As I attempted to calm her down, I reminded her that those who knew her, loved her, and understood her frustrations and also re-educated her on the choices she was making and the implications moving forward. "We've talked about this need for approval and validation Darlene. I recognize that right now you are vulnerable and question many aspects of your life and your decisions. But speaking out on social media for the sole reason of needing reassurance or approval is a damaging way in which to try to get your needs met. In the best-case scenario, you get a verbal "high five" from someone, but that positive feedback isn't enough when it comes to the court of public opinion, especially when using social media as a sounding board during a divorce. I suggested that she grab her journal and write down every thought and feeling that she was experiencing. In the past she had used an application called Penzu, which is an extremely secure journaling site and she loved it because she could create her own designs to personalize her journal, plus it's double locked for security. She had a right to express your feelings, and allow her voice to be heard, but this public forum was not the place for it. This private, protected, and safe place was just right for her.

There may be feelings you haven't felt before as you navigate through this new experience called divorce. Be especially mindful of your emotions when navigating social media. Keep in mind that as you click on your friend's posts, they are showing their best days. They are showing their most attractive days. They are showing you what they want you to see. And most times what is being shown doesn't tell the whole story. And sometimes, when you click on a post that appears to reflect a life that you once had... well it can result in overwhelming feelings of despair and can make you feel as if you are looking back over your shoulder at the familiar life you once had; a life that is now different. We call this perception diluted, or looking through rose-colored glasses. When looking through a distorted lens, we see only partial images, ones that are biased, either positively or negatively. And our perceptions directly impact our mood. You will have good days and bad days as you get through the unknowns of a divorce, and the power of social media is often a direct influence on our mood. Breathe and be mindful of your feelings as you scroll through social media. Even if you start to feel worse, stop, take a breath and a break from whatever site is grabbing your attention.

Over recent years, one of the most common questions my clients posit is whether or not they should unfollow their ex-partner on social media. My client's wonder, "Why is my ex following me? Maybe I should follow them too?" The answer is, "Yes, don't follow them, regardless of whether or not they are following you." I understand the question, although common sense might disagree.

Why in the world would we want to follow them, watch them, or listen to them on social media? It's an interesting question with a simple answer: it's just way too tempting to resist. I would love to be that person who has never cared about what my ex-husband was doing and with whom, but embarrassingly enough, at one point. I did care.

Sharing years of your life with a person, sharing contact with their family and friends and then cutting off connections in the blink of an eye is a difficult task for many newly divorced people. Sometimes, it can feel like it's just too much, especially with social media as an option. But it can go sideways very quickly, and although you may think you're going to feel better, more often than not, you feel lonelier than when you started. When we are thinking clearly, as when we are giving advice to others, we recognize that when it comes to ex-partners, separating ones' lives leads to the healthiest of outcomes. When we have access to personal information about them, our healing process is inhibited by lack of closure, and healing is something we all must do.

Going through a divorce can feel incredibly lonely and isolating, but thankfully, the use of social media can play a positive role in an often difficult and emotionally challenging process. As a therapist facilitating groups across two decades, I am well aware of the healing nature of a support group. When one's own support network is lacking, the connection a group provides can provide a much-needed lifejacket when one is at the mercy of relentless undercurrent of emotions.

Traditionally, groups have been provided in person, with a facilitator leading the group by regulating participation, topics, and group norms. In recent years, this in-person dynamic has been augmented with the availability of many online resources provided to those who may otherwise be unable to attend in person.

As a group member, you can choose to share or to merely listen, depending on your comfort level. Either way, the benefit of a support group is often underestimated. Rarely will you find another venue where you can connect with others who can empathize, relate, and understand what you are going through.

Whether it be via Facebook, MeetUp, or another social media platform, it is through social media that we are able to discover groups that cover a multitude of varying needs, be it a group for single parents, children, or extended family who all may be managing the emotional impact of divorce. Try not to talk yourself out of benefiting from a group experience by thinking that you'll be just fine, or you probably don't need it, because that's not really what a group is about. It isn't about need, it's about people supporting other people in a way that empowers one another. It's not about you being unhealthy, it's about you choosing to stay healthy.

When you find a group, you find a community of people who are there for the same reasons you are—support. Everyday people come together posing questions and solutions for each other. It serves as a reservoir of learning from each other's experiences and is formulated under the guidelines of positive support.

The very first group I ever ran was a women's support group. We met once a week for an hour and half and discussed whatever women's issue the group wanted to hash out at the time. These women were amazing with one another. Their lives were different, their experiences were different, as were their ages, jobs, and marital status. But, their level of empathy and relatability is what made this group so special. They connected on a level that even the closest group of friends struggle to achieve. They "got" each other, and they had each other's back. Their ability to be real, to be vulnerable, and to be fully present for each other created a genuine and long-lasting connection that extended far beyond the reach of my four walls.

Hello Positive Feelings

Believe it or not, we don't just experience negative emotions, we're not one dimensional. I stopped feeling sad after I made the decision to get divorced. My sadness and loneliness occurred pre-divorce, and I felt those feelings intensely. But after I decided to get divorced, I started feeling the good feelings I had been missing, which was a welcome change!

Almost right away I felt relief. I remember getting the best night of sleep that I had in years, after I filed for divorce. I was a single mom, so don't get me wrong, I was exhausted, but I slept great, nonetheless. The thing is, the human body can handle work, even the hardest of work. Hard work is honest and productive. But the emotional turmoil one experiences during the end of a marriage is often the cause of many sleepless nights. As we said before, we aren't wired to tolerate chronic stress. Once relieved of that stress, our bodies slow down, rest, and begin repairing.

Along with relief, you might feel peace. No more arguments, or bickering, or dirty looks. No more wondering what might happen when the both of you are home together. Few things are worse than trying to find excuses to "not go home" and then dreading the drive to your home, which is supposed to be a place of peace and tranquility.

Many women report feeling empowered after divorce. As we all know, women are resilient. We have to be. Female mammals, all mammals, are hard workers. Females are biologically engineered to camouflage into the background, to protect the family. We hunt and gather and protect the young. Often, we forget our resilience, or perhaps it's just that others take what we do for granted. Sometimes we are in the background, providing emotional support. Sometimes we are mediating within our families or running interference. Regardless of your role, most females are busy handling much of everything, with very little credit given. To say that divorce offers an opportunity for empowerment is an understatement. Research has shown that although women after divorce tend to struggle more financially than men, women are also generally happier and more well-balanced. Much of this is due to empowerment. Maybe your husband did all the "heavy lifting" or so it appeared. But now, somehow, the heavy lifting is still being done, even without him around. When I was married and on more than one occasion, I remember receiving notices that checks on my account had bounced. But, after I was divorced and my husband no longer had access to my finances, I never bounced a check again. Somehow, with only having one income to support myself and my son, I never had to pay an "overdraft fee" again. That's empowering.

One of the most positive outcomes of divorce is that of self-awareness. Self-awareness is the knowing of one's emotions.

Life is not a romantic comedy, with a beginning, a middle, and an end. Regardless of the feelings you experience, recognize that emotions don't occur on a timeline. Give yourself time and be patient. All feelings pass, even the good ones. Hopefully, in learning and understanding your feelings, you will find comfort and possibly solace in knowing that this process is a part of the whole of human experience.

CHAPTER 5

Goodbye Carpool Lane

"And one day she discovered that she was fierce, and strong,
and full of fire, and that not even she could hold herself back
because her passion burned brighter than her fears."

— Mark Anthony, The Beautiful Truth

The truth is, you never know what you're capable of until you're forced to do it. But the "doing" isn't always so easy, nor is it usually that simple. Empowerment, responsibility, choice, and one's outlook on life are all critical components of having a pro-active and healthy life. One in which you have the right and responsibility to take care of yourself, all the while setting boundaries and trying to maintain balance. Simple, but not so simple.

To say that going through a divorce is a transition is an understatement. Everything changes, and I mean, everything. Although change is constant, the experience of divorce is an entirely different Oprah episode. But change can be good, and depending on your perception, it is good.

Your world is different now, there's no doubt about it. We joked when I created the title for this chapter, "Goodbye Carpool

Lane," yet the concept is accurate. You're flying solo, without a partner, in your life, in your bed, and in your car. You might have mixed feelings about being alone, and possibly about "not being needed." What's important to remember is that YOU need you, more than anyone else does. Without being able to put your oxygen mask on before you put on the masks of others, it is a surefire way to perish. But, for those of us so attuned to taking care of the needs of others, or even taking a backseat to loved ones, the concept of "where to start" in our own lives might feel slightly elusive.

One of the most honest and healthy outcomes from divorce is empowerment. When push comes to shove, a woman can do anything she sets her mind to—anything. My experience started when my son wanted to have a barbecue with some of his friends over at our house. I had never really barbecued anything, at least not on my own. I knew how to cook, but my ex-husband was the real barbecue chef. Unfortunately, I also realized at that point that my ex-husband had gotten custody of our barbecue in our divorce, and the idea of shopping for a barbecue was daunting, overwhelming, and more than just a little intimidating. So, I did what any savvy shopper in 2017 would do, I ordered one on Amazon. Quick and easy, it arrived the same day! I couldn't believe they could actually deliver a massive item like that so quickly. Didn't they need a truck and a couple guys to help bring it in? When I opened the door, I had expected to see a bright new, shiny, Weber grill. I didn't. What I saw was a rather large box, full of "barbecue pieces." They expected me to put it together. I was dumbfounded. I had absolutely no idea how to do that. I didn't even know how to use one yet, much less put it together.

So, I grabbed my handy neighbor Emily and begged her for help. Being a single mom herself, she was able to relate. And thankfully, she had a toolbox as well. So, we set out on a Saturday afternoon to put our handywoman' talents to work. The job that is supposed to take 45 minutes, according to Amazon reviews, took us about 2 hours, give or take. But when it was done, we were so proud, and very sweaty! We connected the propane and stood back to admire our work. It was at that point that I smelled gas and had absolutely no idea where it was coming from.

So, in reading the directions, because we are women and we do that, we were told that if we smelled gas, we needed to call the fire department. I did not have time for this today. I had to take my son to his football game and really just wanted to leave the darn thing and come back to it later. But, I didn't, and reluctantly I called 911. I told the dispatcher that I had a gas leak and she immediately called out our local firefighters who promptly showed up at my door dressed in hazmat gear. They blazed through my house thinking it was a true gas leak. I was so embarrassed after I told them it was only a barbecue. My son, on the other hand, was grinning ear to ear and couldn't wait to tell his friends about an entire fire department rescuing us during our time of need.

Thankfully they were kind, very cute, and massive. A winning combination. They explained quite patiently to me that it would be wise for me to repair any holes or gaps with Teflon tape. As they saw my eyes glaze over with the mention of this tape, they realized I was absolutely lost. "You mean that stuff they make pots and pans out of?" I asked, trying to repair my ego. They nodded in agreement and jotted down the description and suggested I take it to the hardware store where they were sure I could get the help I needed.

Even though I was more than embarrassed in the moment, in hindsight, my pride and sense of accomplishment were in pretty good shape. After all, two women and a pink toolbox still put together a barbecue all on their own, without one bit of "barbecue knowledge." And, when we needed help with our minor gas leak, we weren't afraid to reach out and ask for assistance. And, as an added bonus, we still had time to put in a couple of hours of baking cookies, and dropped them off into our local fire department along with a big thank you. This time I had a chance to put on lipstick first.

Every time I've had to do something new during my divorce, something clearly out of my comfort zone, I have not only felt accomplished, I've felt empowered. We often talk about empowerment in general terms, without really explaining the meaning or even the course of action behind it. To feel empowered is to feel like you are not only given permission to try to do something you haven't been able to do, but also are able to accomplish that task. There were so many things that I really didn't have access to during my marriage. This wasn't because someone didn't let me, it was because I didn't have enough faith in my ability to try in the first place. I left activities that I thought my husband would be better at, up to my husband to do.

All too often in divorce we interpret events and situations in our marriage and believe them to be true. This is termed confirmation bias. Similar to negativity bias, which is our tendency to recognize negative stimuli more readily and to focus on those events, confirmation bias has its place and is useful for us as humans. As our brain uses confirmation bias as a way to interpret the vast amount of information it is presented with on a daily basis, negativity bias assists us in helping to keep us safe from danger. As humans we tend to see negative data more easily than positive as means of survival. We are hard-wired to look for predators in order to survive. All it takes is one traumatic event and that hard wiring can become a little jaded as the brain remembers the trauma and can often see something as negative as opposed to positive.

The key is to not let our drift toward confirmation bias affect our lives, and more specifically our relationship with ourselves.

The most direct route of attack is our self-esteem. Just because you haven't tried something doesn't mean you are incapable of succeeding. If you're faced with a challenge and are uncertain of your capabilities, before you talk yourself out of it, look for the evidence to support your belief, all of the evidence. Question your judgment of yourself. I was always told by my ex-husband that I didn't have a head for numbers because I didn't use QuickBooks as my bookkeeping platform. While this is true, I'm not quite sure if that meant that I wasn't necessarily "math dumb." I didn't like math, total truth, and I hated spreadsheets. But perhaps his perception of my ability was incorrect. After all, many of his other perceptions of me were inaccurate, which contributed to why we divorced in the first place. Maybe, just maybe, all of my negative self-talk, fueled by the perception of others, was misguided and an incorrect assessment of my left-brain ability. I had to think about that and challenge my confirmation bias.

Empowerment begins with being willing to try something new and keeping an open mind. Even if you're afraid, do it anyway. Think of all of the times you were afraid but pushed ahead regardless of that feeling. Even if it didn't turn out great, or the outcome was a bit of a mess, do you remember that feeling? Sometimes the best choice we have in life is one that we feel we will be less likely to regret. I've never really regretted doing something, but I'm certainly familiar with the feeling of regret when I've held myself back from doing something I was nervous about trying.

Along with "doing" is not being afraid to ask for help. You don't have to be a superwoman, or superhuman. As a single mom I was so accustomed to having to handle things on my own, I often would neglect to ask for help. Whether I would get it or not was another thing. Or maybe it was all a self-fulfilling prophecy. But asking for help can be just as empowering and freeing. We like to help others, why wouldn't someone else feel the same feeling of being valued or needed when we ask for their help. Asking for assistance doesn't mean you're not capable, it just means you're secure enough to make yourself vulnerable. It's important to remember that asking for help doesn't mean that you need to forego your boundaries. Boundaries are still and always in play, no matter what.

When we think of the term responsibility, we might think of it as "one more thing we have to do." But, in reality, responsibility is empowerment. The value of not seeing yourself as a victim and empowering yourself to take accountability for your actions, is priceless. Even if you were on the receiving end of a bitter breakup, and truly you were victimized, this is very different from viewing yourself as a victim. If wrongdoing has been done to you, then you were victimized, and there's no denying that. Working with survivors of sexual assault over the past 22 years, they are just that "survivors." Were they victimized, absolutely. But being a victim is not who they are. When something is done TO you, it doesn't then define who you are. That awful act doesn't have that much power. The power to change your actual being. Nothing is that powerful.

"Do not let the behavior of others destroy your inner peace."
—Dalai Lama

Work on achieving balance by saying "no." One of my favorite books, "When I say no, I feel guilty" summarizes beautifully how difficult it is for us to say no because of our extreme discomfort with the feeling of guilt. But if you are truly working on achieving balance in your life, then learning to say no is a necessity. Saying "no" is not as easily accepted in our society as saying "yes." As young children we are taught to respect authority, be polite, and to not cause conflict. These are the beliefs we later carry into our adult lives. We tend to want to avoid conflict, to fit in, and to have people like us. We don't want to disappoint others as this adds to our fear of rejection.

We use disclaimers or justifications, which we feel we need to use to defend our reason for saying no. Unfortunately, all this does is make your choice to say "no" look weaker and you tend to lose credibility. At the end of the day, we want people to respect our choice to say no, and to not view it as suspicious or malevolent.

Saying no may be especially difficult for women as we are taught that it is better to be viewed as flexible and compliant rather than being seen as a bitch. I remember attending a conference where Brené Brown was conducting a break-out session and the topic was Overcoming Guilt and Shame. Brené's story started with her stating that as a mom, living in the South, certain things were expected of her. For example, she was expected to participate in her daughter's school fundraiser and often felt pressured to bake chocolate chip cookies as part of said fundraiser. This request came every year from the chairwoman herself. Unfortunately, Brené not only disliked chocolate chip cookies, she also didn't care for the chairwoman. But, year after year, rather than saying "no" to this request, she begrudgingly said "yes." But that year she vowed that it would be different. She had purchased a new ring, just for her 40th birthday, and while holding on to that ring she pledged to spin it three times while saying "choose discomfort over resentment" and then after the third time, she would have the strength to say no. And so she did. Shockingly, her discomfort was short lived and even more surprisingly, her response was met with "no problem" and a wave goodbye. What Brené Brown learned that day was that any discomfort she felt was probably greater than the discomfort she was initially sure she would be imparting on the receiver.

But saying "no" is extremely difficult, because, being social beings, we all have the innate need to be accepted by our peer group.

So how do you start practicing using your voice without feeling more uncomfortable than necessary?

Starting with practicing saying "no" is a minor situation. For example, when asked in a store if you like to join their shopping club or apply for a card, say "no" without using any disclaimers or justifications. Remember that, although saying no might feel uncomfortable in the moment, this is only short-term discomfort. It is highly unlikely that you will ever see this person again, even if you wanted to. But the verbal beating we often endure in the space of our own minds when we ignore our gut can feel relentless, "You know you should have said no, why didn't you do that?" That long term discomfort feels far less tolerable than the immediate negative feeling you might experience in the moment. Is it really worth it?

Take a minute and assess the situation. If you're afraid of being rejected or disliked, ask yourself the question "If someone was saying 'no' to me in this situation, would I consider it reasonable? Would I be angry with them merely because they turned me down?"

More often than not, the idea of saying no is far worse than the actual act. The what ifs can wreak havoc on our overactive minds. When it comes to anxiety, it's important to remember two very critical rules. Number one, it's never going to be as bad as you think. And number two, you are always going to overestimate danger. Ask yourself these questions: "Can I handle the feelings I might have as a result?" and "How bad could it be?"

For many of us, the thought of putting ourselves first is far from automatic, and consequently takes practice. Start by taking baby steps in prioritizing yourself, and carve out time just for you. Divorce is more than time consuming. It's draining on many levels, and when you're in the throes of it, our own needs tend to fall by the wayside. But "me time" is critical for your mental health. This time doesn't necessarily need to be solitary. Although time alone is very important, sometimes too much time alone can lead to isolation and consequently, depression. Be mindful of having a healthy balance between time solo as well as time with others. Make a list of things you haven't tried but have always wanted to. Maybe it's a cooking class, or a book club, or a hiking group. Try to think outside of the box. Pay attention to parts of your life that you might have been neglecting. For example, maybe you haven't worked out in a while, or haven't seen friends or extended family. Make an effort to realign yourself with the things you enjoy, while also trying new experiences.

In addition to focusing on time for yourself, implement the right space for yourself as well. Try to make your environment more of a reflection of you. I remember a client once telling me that the first thing she bought after her divorce "dust" was settled, was a new bed and sheets. I thought this was a no-brainer, but when I went through my divorce, I noticed I needed to actually give myself permission to buy "new things", including a new bed. It was difficult for me to justify, especially being a single mom, the spending of any money as the cost of my divorce wasn't cheap by any stretch. But the second I allowed myself to make my environment more "Michelle-like" was the second I felt like I was starting a new life.

It doesn't have to be a big expenditure. But it should be something that is you. Maybe it's an item your ex-spouse would've thought was frivolous or didn't value as much as you. Whatever it is, buy it for yourself. Allow yourself to remove the cobwebs of your old life and begin making a new one for yourself. Your home is an extension of you, and now that it isn't a source of conflict, it should be one that is a source of comfort. A new plant, a piece of art, a dish set, a pink toolbox, let yourself have it without questioning the purchase.

Focus on yourself. It's time to figure out other ways in which to meet your needs, in your own way, and in your own style. If you're like me, and a mom, you might've forgotten what you used to enjoy before you married, and became a mother. I remember the first time my son went away with his dad for an adventure guided weekend trip. I was so excited because I had the entire weekend to myself. And then I thought, "What do I like to do?" Honestly, I couldn't remember. Everything I had done until that point seemed centered either around my husband or my son, or both. Whatever used to keep me so busy prior to getting married, was completely off my radar. I found myself eager for my son to return home. This was not the best, nor the healthiest use of my "me" time.

Become reacquainted with your own values and sense of self. One of the best tools I've used in my therapy practice is that of the Life Map. The most important part of doing a life map is the focus on self-reflection. How you perceive your past has a direct impact on your present life and can influence the story of your future. If your life story isn't what you want, or hasn't been, then creating a life map is an extremely useful tool in helping to create a new narrative as you are the author of your future.

The fascinating thing about a life map is that it invites us to observe and engage our own lives from multiple perspectives. Imagine yourself hovering from above and looking down at your world, and your life, from the sky. Stepping back and observing from a distance helps you see the bigger picture and often a clearer path. Unlike seeing the forest for the trees.

By gazing into my past, present, and future, my reflections offer me an opportunity to remember and validate my identity formation, and intentionally reflect on who I was, who I am, and who I hope to be.

You might feel an abundance of emotions as you examine and reflect. Take a breath and try to be in the moment, without judgment.

LIFE MAP ACTIVITY

A life map is just that, a map of your life. It includes symbols and pictures that reflect your life. The experiences from your past, present and future are recorded to provide a visual representation of your life's journey.

PART 1: THOUGHTFUL PREPARATION

1. Set aside 30 minutes to an hour to contemplate your life. You can always do more if you choose; this is just a general guideline to thoughtfully reflect on the course of your life, its highs, lows, and stable times.

PART 2: BRAINSTORM

1. What might have been some key obstacles in your life? Challenges, interpersonal struggles, etc. Who are the characters, significant people, or relationships in your life?

2. What have been some Milestone Successes in your life? These are things that you might be proud of. For example, these might be the "green lights" of life, the pleasant surprises, which have given you happiness or peace. A green light is a sign that it's okay to proceed ahead.

Write Everything Down

1. Go ahead and just list out as many things as you can from your brainstorm while keeping in mind the guidelines below. Include experiences that influenced your life and later successes, both positive and negative.

2. Be mindful of significant life events, those that occur approximately every other year or so. For example, if you are 30 to 40 years old, you might have 15 to 20 life events.

3. If you notice yourself including more negative events than positive, do note that for your later reflections after you've finished drawing your life map. If you notice yourself putting in more positive ones, please also note this in your reflections too.

4. Imagine your life story as a novel; think of your life story (life map) in terms of plots and characters, along with all the different factors that may have influenced who you are today. For example, this might include major decisions that took you on a new path, or challenging choices that took you on a road less traveled. The small choices that led to unexpected discoveries. Document the impact of important relationships, goals, beliefs, and even aspects of human behavior have had in your life. Please feel free to add or take away as you wish. This list is merely a suggestion to help with the process.

5. Try to put the events in chronological order. Note down your (approximate) age at the time of a given event. If it is difficult to recall, try to imagine other events in the same timeline. This may help connect the dots of time a bit better.

6. Identify the positive and negative events. Add a "+" sign in front of events that are overall positive, and a "−" sign in front of ones that you perceive as overall negative—and then rate the positive or negative intensity of each event on a scale of 1 to 10, low to high. If it feels genuinely neutral, simply put in an "n" or a "0".

PART 3: DRAW YOUR LIFE MAP

1. Create a road or path, mapping out all of your life events along the way. It can be windy, or straight, depending on how you have viewed your life journey.

2. Indicate your positive and negative experiences by continuing the use of symbols, such as + or –, or express yourself by using colors that indicate either something positive or negative.

3. Use pictures, symbols, or words as you create a "visual narrative" to your life map. Stop signs, roadblocks, obstacles, or pathways are usual ways to represent opportunities, or problems, on life's path.

4. Get creative and feel free to draw simple or elaborate pictures to illustrate where you've been in your life, and where you might see yourself going.

PART 4: NEXT STEPS: REFLECTING ON YOUR LIFE MAP

Here are some questions to reflect on:

- What has influenced the choices you make?
- What has helped you move forward and make progress?
- What has moved you backward?
- Do you see life as a journey? If so, why? If not, how else do you see it?

CHAPTER 6.

Hello Beautiful

I remember the day that my son first realized I wasn't just "Michael's mom." It was a Saturday evening, an evening in which he would be with his dad. I had made plans to go out with friends and we were meeting a little earlier than usual. I never really made plans to go out without my son unless he was with his father. Since we alternated weekends, it was fairly easy to make plans when he was elsewhere. This particular Saturday, his father was a little late, so I needed to prepare myself while he was at home. A few minutes before his dad arrived, I joined him and his friends outside while they were playing a game of "two on two" and the oldest boy in the bunch blurted out, "Where are you going?" My son immediately replied with, "She's not going anywhere. I'm going to my dad's, so she is staying home." His friend, who was about 3 years his senior and a very knowledgeable boy of about 13 laughed, and said, "Yeah right. She's not staying home looking like that!" For a hot second, I felt like I was busted. They both looked at me as I fumbled my words like a girl getting caught sneaking in after curfew. "Oh, I'm just going to maybe run to the store or grab a bite to eat, nothing major." Clearly this wasn't true, nor did I have a reason to lie. I was a grown woman who was entitled to have a life, a kind of life I wanted, and it was no one's business but my own. But I felt embarrassed, caught doing something wrong, cheating on my son, or some other mortal sin I couldn't pinpoint at that moment. In my nakedness I knew I wasn't feeling confident, and I realized that needed to change.

I suppose I was so used to being a wife, a mom, a breadwinner, that there really wasn't any time to be a woman. I knew I needed to start feeling like a woman again. Not a mom, and certainly not a wife, but a woman. I knew I was all of those things, and more, I just wasn't connected to myself the way I once had been. It's difficult to describe losing oneself. Although I was able to throw on a dress and put on some makeup, my body image was lacking, my personal self-care was basic, and I had become quite deft at either pushing aside or concealing my emotions. I missed feeling "pretty." It seems like a simple, maybe trivial thing, but I missed the way I felt when I felt pretty. And by that I don't mean physically necessarily, just the feeling of pretty. My son certainly didn't see me as anything other than "mom" and my spouse hadn't seen me at all for years. I knew I was tired of feeling like an afterthought, and that I was the only one who could bring me back to life.

Shopping was easy. Since it had been ages since I had been on an actual "date," even with my husband, clothes were either professional attire or yoga pants, sometimes one and the same. Lululemon was my go-to shopping spot, but that wasn't good enough anymore. It wasn't good enough for me. Before I was married, and when I was dating, I dressed for my dates, not so much myself. I bought and wore what I thought THEY might like, not necessarily what made me feel good. More often than not, we see these as being one in the same, but that couldn't be further from the truth. Dressing for someone else shoots confidence in the foot, and confidence is sexy.

And let's talk about undergarments. I wore them, but they weren't pretty. They were basic, comfortable, so not sexy. When I went through my drawers, I realized I hadn't worn anything sexy in years, not that any of my prior "sexy-ware" would fit anyway. I needed pretty panties and bras that actually fit me. And I needed them for me, not for anyone else. I needed to feel sexy, to be sexy, and to believe that I was sexy. I needed to put the time into that. And it needed to be more than the 15 minutes a day I allowed for my hair which included wrapping up the wet mess in a bun, plus an extra 10 minutes for mascara and lipstick. That wasn't going to cut it anymore. Maybe it was okay for mommy, but not for my goal of reconnecting with my sensual, female, and amazing self, at least for every other Saturday and alternating Wednesdays.

I imagined my old self, prior to marriage, and began with an inventory of what mattered to me, what piqued my interest, what I used to do, and how I used to feel when I was single. I looked at photos to re-spark my memory of the "old me" just to become re-acquainted. I realized, for starters, that my body image needed a makeover, from the inside out. I was physically weak, and I knew it. I had torn my rotator cuff when I was 30 years old, and my upper body strength wasn't anywhere it used to be. Plus, my son, who was big enough to carry himself, still demanded I carry him to and from the beach, and yes, to my own detriment, I enabled him. But he was getting bigger.

I used to go to the gym, and I used to run. Both of those sounded very unappealing to me. The last thing I wanted was to get my butt out of my warm bed at the crack of dawn and go for a run or hit the gym. I just knew I wouldn't do it. But a friend of mine recommended Pilates. I took a free class, and after that I was hooked. For me, it was my own religion. For one hour a day I was allowed to be mindful and present, and truly in the moment. And I loved it. I slowly regained my strength and began to recognize little muscles on my arms and legs. I couldn't believe that something I enjoyed so much could actually create a physical change, which was a bonus.

I recall the first time I met Veronica. She was an older woman, about 10 years my senior. She had just gotten divorced for the second time, and realized that relationships really weren't for her. I had no judgment about this, her life was her own to live. But her connection with herself was lacking, which is why she came to therapy. She had always been a very active woman, more active than her age would ever indicate. But when her former husband had become sick, she dedicated all of her time to his care. After they divorced, she was lost. She didn't have him to care for, and her sense of self was missing. Our goal in therapy was to help her reconnect with her own sense of purpose, passion, self. The day she signed up for a dance class was the day I realized she was on the right track to self-awareness. She had always been a dancer, and had a dancer's body. The movement was just natural for her. It made her feel sensual, beautiful, passionate, and free.

I remember thinking "I cannot even think about dating again" on more than one occasion during the process of my divorce. And then there was the idea of sex. Although we are sexual beings, during the final years before the end of my marriage, sex was pretty non-existent. When it did occur, it felt obligatory, or mechanical. Unfortunately, sexual desire is derived from frequent sexual experiences, and without that, our libido wanes. Out of practice, out of mind. And for at least a couple of years, it was truly out of my mind. I remember thinking, "I'm pretty sure I'm still capable, or maybe my hymen has actually grown back! Who knew?!" Were the positions still the same, was there something new being done that I was completely unaware of? Did I need to watch a video? Were there still videos? There was so much to consider, it was almost overwhelming.

After considerable over-thinking, I got past the idea that I may not really know how my girl parts worked anymore. It has been so long since I have been vulnerable intimately, even with myself. I didn't know what I liked anymore. I had spent so many years trying to take care of the needs of others, I just had no idea what mine were. Intimacy, sex, foreplay, cuddling, it felt all so foreign.

I think I had a vibrator somewhere, but I was pretty sure it was riddled with cobwebs. Maybe it was mixed up with the Christmas ornaments by mistake. That's all I needed—my rabbit vibrator co-habitating with the Elf on a Shelf.

Before I ended up further down the rabbit hole, pardon the pun, I thought of Elizabeth's Taylor's famous line, "Pour yourself a drink, put on some lipstick, and pull yourself together."

Your sexuality is as individual as you are, and the sexual experience you have with yourself is the most important relationship you will ever have. Don't compare yourself to others or allow society to dictate how you should or shouldn't behave. When you compare yourself to others, or allow others' opinions to affect who you are and how you behave, you essentially cripple yourself. You shoot a bullet right through your self-esteem and shatter your confidence. Others will have opinions, they always do. Typically, these opinions are self-serving, biased, and channeled through the lens of projection. Projection is essentially the feelings others have about themselves and their situations, projected onto others. Typically, if someone has a strong opinion about you or what you are doing, that opinion is a projection of their own thoughts and feelings about themselves. Unfortunately, projections are typically negative and can often be sabotaging. There's a saying, "If someone points a finger at you, notice that three other fingers are pointing back at them." Listening to the unsolicited feedback of others can kill a budding seed before it has had a chance to grow. It's your job to protect that seed and to nurture it. It's your job to allow yourself the opportunity to blossom into the amazing and very unique woman that you are.

I realized that when it came to sex and men, the most important thing was that I was and am a female, and all a guy really cares about is whether or not I show up. I was then able to take a breath just in time for a new wave of anxiety to hit me. I don't make the best decisions when it comes to men and I was in no position to make a wise choice in a partner, I wasn't ready for a new partner, or any real relationship, and when oxytocin kicks in, all my good judgment goes out the window.

Oxytocin is often referred to as the "cuddling or love hormone." Oxytocin is produced in the hypothalamus and is released during sex, childbirth, and breastfeeding. The release of oxytocin stimulates the womb and creates lactation. The biological role of this hormone is to create attachment. While oxytocin is the main hormone released during sex for women, men experience a higher increase in dopamine, which elicits pleasure. After orgasm, the level of Oxytocin in a woman's body stays elevated, whereas a man's dopamine level decreases. Suffice to say it is speculated, due to the differences in the release of these hormones during sex, that women tend to become more attached, regardless as to whether or not their partner is worthy of attachment, than their male counterparts. Therein lies the conundrum. How does a woman hope to experience intimacy, pleasure, and sexual gratification from being with a man, without becoming attached to him?

Since I was clearly long overdue for intimacy, I needed to have a plan. So, I came up with one: I was going to date younger men, I mean significantly younger. My logic was this: If I go out with someone 10 or more years younger than me, then I know for sure I won't plan on sharing my life with him, hence no risk of attachment. It seemed safe to say this was the best way for me to not talk myself into liking someone who wouldn't be right for me. I didn't say it was an ideal plan, but it was the best I could come up with while honoring my wants and trying not to repeat my past lack of judgment-based decisions, i.e., "looking for love in all the wrong places."

I had no problem calling myself a cougar, at least silently to myself. I know many women reading this might take issue with the term, but I had no problem with it. My sexuality at the time had been so repressed in marriage, I was just starting to become sexually self-aware again. I wanted to discover and explore my wants, recognize and respect my libido, and get to know my body with respect to being intimate with a man again. I missed sex terribly. I didn't realize it until I realized it, until I had a moment to think about myself first rather than everyone else in my life. I could still be a mom, and be a woman, right?? I crossed my fingers and held my breath once again.

I can't deny what I wanted, and what I truly enjoy and appreciate. Men want what women want. They want a connection, they want to be appreciated, they want to be understood, and they want to feel attractive.

I shared my "wants" with a newly single girlfriend who truly understood. She was the one who educated me about the various dating applications available, specifically Bumble. This dating application is one in which you download and post a very, very brief profile and a few pictures, and voila, you're on the market. The difference between *Bumble* and other applications like *Tinder* and *Hinge* is that the woman has to make the first contact. I had no problem with this, especially since it was only virtual, and I also developed a catchy introduction… "At the risk of sounding too blunt, you're sexy as hell." I realize it sounds a little aggressive, but men ate it up.

Most men, it turns out, are not used to women initiating at all, much less by using the word "sexy" in an intro. So, my intro worked like a charm, at least for the desired goal at the time. It opened the door to opportunities to meet men who were attractive, interesting, and very flattering. It made me feel like a woman again and that was a very, very good feeling. I didn't need to be a wife, a mom, or a business owner. I didn't have to try to impress anyone, I just had to be female and open to the experience of getting to know someone, allowing someone to compliment me, make me laugh, and get me excited again.

If you've ever had kids, you know that even the best mom in the world is rarely appreciated as much as she deserves to be. It's not until many years later that kids understand and appreciate everything a mom does, and I'm still waiting. And my soon-to-be-ex-husband at the time, well, let's just say appreciative comments had fallen by the wayside many years ago. So being with someone who wanted to do things for me, didn't take me for granted, and who saw me as a vibrant woman, was a very welcome addition to my already rather full life.

I met some very nice, very interesting, and very sexy men. I tried not to define my type, after all I really didn't know what my type was exactly. I learned how to "meet" men all over again, as an older woman who is supposed to have her shit together. The "shit together" part is a work in progress. I found my inner-female and discovered she wasn't hidden that far inside, she just needed the right incentive, the right encouragement, and the right reinforcement. Once I realized what I had been missing for many years, especially toward the end of my marriage, I vowed to never forget how important intimacy, and it's not always sex, is to me as a woman and as a human being. And my sexual partner, well it's oxytocin... go figure. That partner is reliable, fulfilling on many levels and never fails to make me feel good, sometimes repeatedly. What else could a woman want? At least until she's ready for more.

In my professional practice I've worked with many women who have struggled in their personal relationships with men and in their ability to recognize their own needs separate from the needs of their partners. Many times, the stories are very similar: A woman meets a man, a man displays interest, is attentive, and pursues her until the point in which he knows she's interested. At that point she is hooked, so to speak. He continues to display interest until he doesn't any longer. She wonders what she did wrong. She thinks, "I must have done something wrong, right?" I mean he was interested, so very interested, but now he's distant. What did I do?" And then she tries everything to fix it, to fix her. One of the problems with this plan is that the more work we put into something, whatever it is, the more valuable that thing becomes, without any effort on its part. But, it's so very difficult to believe that whatever changed in a man's heart isn't about anything that you did. What you don't realize is that you didn't do anything at all. He was interested, very much so, and then he wasn't any longer. It had nothing to do with her making him no longer interested. It wasn't meant to be, for whatever reason.

One of the differences between men and women, at least when we look at societal roles, is that men seem to be able to, at least a little more easily, just enjoy the presence of a woman, without necessarily wanting to see her again. For many women, this is very difficult to comprehend. We tend to think, "If he enjoys being with me so much, why wouldn't he want it to last?" And maybe they do want it to last, at least in that moment. Men often tend to be more comfortable in the present, in the moment, not necessarily planning for the future. They want the same thing, but they tend to think about it differently, from more of a "one step at a time" perspective. In working with many men and women over the years, specifically couples, I've discovered that this can be a major barrier in communication. Although their goals are aligned, the thought patterns can differ, which often leads to miscommunication and lack of understanding, and sometimes, hurt feelings. Of course, there are always exceptions and not all men or women are the same, by any means.

I remember the day my client Monica walked into my office first thing on a Monday morning, visually upset after a long week of obsessing. The prior week she had gone on a date with a new guy and had an amazing time. It was their first date, but she felt an immediate connection. "Right away I knew we both felt it—the chemistry I mean. We even laughed about the fact that we had been on dates where it was clear, chemistry was non-existent, and that makes for a very long evening. I think we were both so relieved that the feeling was mutual immediately. The evening just naturally flowed. We agreed on almost everything. After dinner, we went for a drink, and just chatted away like we had known each other forever." I was confused as to why she was so upset since she clearly had a wonderful first date. "You're confused?" She asked. "I'm confused as well!" Apparently, at this point it had been almost a week and she hadn't heard from him. "After we hugged goodnight, we agreed that it would be great to see each other again. And since then, nothing. No call, no text, just crickets."

Although Monica said she knew it wasn't about her, what she believed was very different. She felt like he had "faked" his interest in her, played her, and led her on. Perhaps this was true. But that's not about her. That's more about him. If that was truly his agenda, then she dodged a bullet. But telling her this did nothing to change her feelings about herself. It only made her feel dumb in believing his intentions. She blamed herself.

It took considerable convincing and reminding that she had said she had an amazing time. That there was chemistry between them, and that is quite difficult to fake. I asked her if it was possible that a great first date isn't a promise for a second one. We often get caught up in the moment, especially on the heels of bad experiences, and that excitement is more emotional than intellectual. It is then, after the dust settles that our rational brains can kick in and allow us to think through the next step. She didn't really know him, not really. She knew what he presented, what he shared, but not really him. Who knows why he didn't contact her again. She didn't really need to know why; she needed reassurance that it wasn't her. She was still the amazing woman she was at the beginning of the date, the middle, and the end. Nothing changes that.

When I'm working with my clients professionally, I explain that it truly isn't personal, that saying "It's not you, it's me," can be, and often is, the truth. But we do need to protect our hearts, the best that we can. The best and most important way to protect yourself is to get to know yourself and what tends to affect you in ways that, realistically, probably won't ever change. If you know that after you become intimate with a man, you become emotionally invested, then it's often best to wait until you feel it's going to last. This is understandably difficult, the power of oxytocin puts us at its mercy, just as dopamine sends a man to his knees.

It's important to have and live your own life and an intimate partner can be a part of that life, but that person can never be more important than you are to yourself. Not ever. And the truth is that the right kind of partner wants you to have a life, it makes you more interesting. You should want your own fulfilling life as well.

Knowing yourself, so that you can be yourself, is the first step. You're a woman, you're special and it's so very important to know that. Treating yourself like you matter is crucial. Making a commitment to yourself, much in the way that you commit to others, reminds you of just how valuable you are.

CHAPTER 7.

Single: I Could Get Used to This

The first loving relationship after divorce, should be with yourself.

One of the most common triggers that brings new clients to therapy is that of a breakup. If you're on the receiving end of the news, you are devastated. Rejection, confusion, anger, or all of the above, feels unbearable. Maybe you weren't ready, were blindsided, felt betrayed, or led on. Or maybe you saw it coming but were cocooned in denial, just hoping that your relationship would get back on track and would be salvageable. And as anyone who's ever been on the receiving end of a breakup knows, that rejection and loss of a partner leaves wounds so painful, they almost feel unhealable. The fact that over time, not only will you recover, but that you might even be grateful that it didn't last, seems like a fantasy. And the idea of being single feels like the punchline of a bad joke. "I don't want to be single! I want him," is something I've heard on many occasions, and repeated myself at various junctures in my own life.

Being the initiator of a breakup comes with its own level of distress. Choosing to end a relationship, regardless of whether the relationship is healthy or not, takes a tremendous amount of courage. Essentially, the fear of making the wrong choice is what tends to send our emotions into a tailspin. As we discussed in prior chapters, we are creatures of habit, and we don't like change. We will choose being comfortable in the "known" hands over fist above the "unknown." The truth is, I have never heard anyone, either professionally or personally say, "Wow, I should've never ended that relationship." But I can't count how many times I have heard, "I can't believe I stayed so long."

Whether it's a divorce, or a long term committed relationship, when that break finally happens, however it transpires, a world of new experiences, relationships, and adventures opens up. It might take some time to heal, to realize that your partner wasn't really the "best part of your life," but, eventually, when you've moved past the heartbreak and are at peace with the ending of the relationship, the reality of being single is a breath of newfound freedom. Your new "singlehood" could also be the start of the best relationship of your life.

Divorce is about a new beginning, not a failed marriage. It's merely the ending of one chapter and the beginning of another. As a newly single woman, you now have the privilege to learn about yourself, and embrace this opportunity to grow. The future is brighter than you think.

The Beauty of Being Single

According to the U.S. Census Bureau, approximately 45% of all Americans over the age of 18, are single. Not only has this number been increasing since 2015, but people are also staying single longer than ever before, with the median age for first time marriages being 30 years for men, and 28 years of age for women. So, if you are single, you are far from being alone.

Given the significant number of singles in this country, it is shocking that the stigma in society is that a single woman is not single by choice, but by necessity. Society still tends to view a single woman as lonely, bitter, and often desperate. She wants to be in a relationship, but despite her best efforts, has been unable to find Mr. Right. How many times have I heard these words tumble out of someone's unfiltered mouth, "Oh, you're single. Don't worry, I'm sure the right guy is out there for you somewhere. Don't give up." The belief that a woman would choose to be single is one that society has yet to embrace. Sadly, our society still views being single as a place of purgatory in which one is merely waiting until the next potential partner comes along.

The truth is, being single allows you the freedom to redefine yourself, on your own terms. It doesn't mean that you are without a partner due to some failure on your part.

To say that being single can strengthen your quality of life is not to say that being married does the opposite. On the contrary. The point is that being single can and should be a choice, and a healthy one at that. It is often because of society's stigmas toward women who are single, that many women feel compelled to be in relationships either married or committed, thereby eliminating the choice in lieu of social acceptance. Whether it be at a restaurant, a concert, or a vacation, the default in society is a party of two, not the woman flying solo. And if she happens to be alone, well that is rarely perceived as a choice.

Prior to my marriage, I didn't feel lonely until someone pointed a finger and implied that I should feel lonely since I was without a partner. As I felt the face of judgment glare upon me, I genuinely started to believe that something was wrong with me because I wasn't married yet. I was in my 30s, and apparently to many I was getting past my prime, inching closer to my expiration date.

I recall being a 28-year-old, over-extended graduate student needing to schedule my yearly women's wellness exam. Since my insurance was Kaiser, which is an HMO network plan, my physician was typically whomever happened on the staff schedule that day. Normally that wouldn't have been a big deal for me, however this day was different in that this would be the first time I would have a male physician. The exam itself went smoothly enough, but what didn't run so smoothly was the conversation that occurred after my appointment; nothing would have prepared me for that. My doctor was not only male, but a very old male OBGYN, presumably inching closely toward his own expiration date. His opening statement appeared benign enough. "Miss, do you plan on having children?" I answered, "Yes, I do." "Well, you are 28 years old I see here." Hmmm, so far he was still playing fairly, but I was beginning to feel myself become hot and mildly uncomfortable. "Do you have a boyfriend?" Now, he was teetering over a boundary. "I don't," I said. "Well," he responded, "I'd advise you to begin working on that as your eggs are getting older and you don't have much time left." I felt sick. I didn't know what to say, so I just mumbled, "Okay" and left. Feeling like I had failed at every relationship and was doomed to a life without children because I didn't have a boyfriend at age 28, I cried the entire 40-minute drive home. How could I have screwed up my life so badly by choosing grad school over starting a life plan of getting married and then having children? It wasn't until later that night that I realized he was flat out wrong. Not only did he bulldoze through my boundaries, his behavior was borderline unethical. My choices were mine, right or wrong, and he had no right to share his opinion without an invitation. The next day, I found my voice and filed a complaint against him, and thankfully, it was taken seriously. He had abused a position in which he was expected to show compassion by replacing it with judgment. In the years that followed, I shared this story with many clients and younger friends who have experienced the same disapproval or condemnation at the hands of authority figures in the medical community. Their judgment is more about them than it is anyone else. Your life's journey is a personal one, one in which your choices are your own.

As I reflect on that experience, I wonder how often women are placed in a position where they feel pressured, so much so that they marry the wrong person. And if society was able to evolve and refrain from its judgment, how many people might stay single for the right reason, thereby freeing up others to marry for the right reason? Wouldn't that benefit both populations?

In a recent study, more than 79,000 women were studied over a three-year-period as they stayed unmarried; got married or entered a relationship that was like marriage; stayed married; or got divorced or separated. The study discovered, with just one exception, every difference in physical health favored people who either stayed single or got divorced. (Dinour, L. Leung, M.M., Tripiccio G. Khan, 2012). Moreover, according to the most recent, and well-respected, longitudinal research studies conducted by London's Kingston University, women become much more satisfied and happier up to five years after their divorce. (*Science Daily*. 10 July 2013). If our happiness and life satisfaction is not contingent on our relationship status, then why all of the pressure to couple up?

Identifying the true reasons why married or single people are or aren't happy in their current situations is far more complicated than the research presents. For starters, when we examine the reasons for life dissatisfaction, we recognize a discrepancy between what we have and what we think we should have. The pressures of society to "couple up" and the stigma placed on those who are single affects many by contributing to a phenomenon that we term "the wanting effect." One moment you are happy, satisfied, and fulfilled in your single life and the next you're feeling the disapproval of society, the impression that there must be something wrong with you for choosing this life, and that you should be wanting more.

At this stage, feelings of disappointment and frustrations are likely to become salient. Societal pressures are a significant compounding factor when it comes to the conflict between "wants and haves." For example, when it comes to consumerism, in our Westernized society we are constantly reminded of what others have compared to what we have, which prevents us from merely appreciating our current situation. Reminded, or even pressured to have something else tends to pull you away from being happy with what you have and refocuses instead on what is missing.

Renowned researcher on the topic of single people, Bella DePaulo, PhD, whose mission is to re-educate and cast doubt on the myth that single people are less happy than their married counterparts, believes it's only a matter of time before these stereotypes begin to fade. "I do think that as the number of single people continues to grow—to well over 100 million adults just in the U.S.—it will be increasingly difficult to maintain the stereotypes and caricatures of single people," says DePaulo. "There are just too many single people who are happy and healthy and love their single lives, and too many people who know single people who are thriving, for the misperceptions to endure."

Her advice is simple, yet easily forgotten so often by us, "Living your single life fully, joyfully, and unapologetically—even as other people are insisting, without any good scientific basis, that you must be less healthy in your choices—is a good way to maintain your good health." DePaulo, B. "What no one ever told you about people who are single." YouTube, uploaded by TED. May 11, 2017. https://youtu.be/lyZysfafOAs

But a healthy and happy single individual doesn't just "happen." Like anything in life, it takes work. But the work is an investment, much like your marriage was at one time. Investing in your relationship with yourself through improving your quality of life is likely to provide a higher return than any other on the market.

I remember when my client Barbara decided that being married just wasn't for her. She had never been married, but had one son that she had given birth to when she was 25 years old. When her son's father made the decision to no longer participate in either of their lives, she set out to raise him on her own. She became engaged 10 years later, but sadly, her fiancé was killed in a motorcycle accident. Understandably, she was devastated. Her grieving process lasted many years, and the loss of him was almost more than she could stand. But eventually she healed, and was able to move past the trauma. When she stepped into my office, at age 40, it was at the prompting of her family who were concerned about her decision to stay single with no plan in finding a partner. "I'm not interested in dating, not really, and I'm just now starting to appreciate and enjoy my life after the loss of Barry. If I'm not bothered by my single status, why should they be?" That was indeed a fair question. Her son was now a teenager, and was very involved in his own life, and for the first time he was needing very little from her. "As a single mom all of these years, this is the first chance I have really had to just focus on myself. I've become very close to two of my girlfriends, closer than even my family I think. I'm not alone, not really. My neighbors and I are a tight-knit group, and meet twice a week for dinner. I'm in a regular yoga class that I love, and I'm planning a yoga retreat with my girlfriends this Fall." I was impressed at her level of commitment to herself, and her interpersonal community. She looked and sounded happy, for the first time in a very long time. "Why would I want to experience the loss I experienced years ago?" I responded, "Barbara, I hope your fear of loss is not what is preventing you from dating." Thankfully, she convinced me that wasn't the case. "It's not that at all. My life is not only fulfilling, but actually filled with the love and companionship of those closest to me. We take care of each other so I'm really not needing or wanting anything else." It was difficult to dispute that. Truthfully, I agreed with her. That is really what all of us should want, but not what all of us have. Barabara's family was concerned, just as I was, that fear was holding Barbara prisoner and preventing her from finding love again. The truth was that she had found it already with those closest to her and her cup was full. Her reciprocal relationships were more than enough to provide her with the joy and togetherness that many of us desire.

People want to feel needed; we all want to feel like someone needs us, and although people feel that they might be a burden on friends, the contrary is true. In addition, without the vulnerability that accompanies asking for support, relationships are more superficial, lacking the depth that vulnerability provides. In 2015, researchers Natalia Sarkisian and Naomi Gerstel discovered that single people are more likely to keep in contact with and receive assistance from friends, family, and neighbors than those who are married. Married people tend to rely more heavily on their partners for support. Sarkisian, N., & Gerstel, N. (2016). Does singlehood isolate or integrate? Examining the link between marital status and ties to kin, friends, and neighbors. Journal of Social and Personal Relationships, 33(3), 361–384. https://doi.org/10.1177/0265407515597564.

As a whole, people who are single place a significant priority on interpersonal relationships and tend to have more time to develop stronger friendships, thereby increasing social connections. Their social networks tend to be broader and more encompassing. Moreover, the better one is at cultivating platonic relationships, the higher the likelihood that they will have healthier and stronger romantic relationships.

Single people who thrive, also truly know how to embrace their solitude. We all need time alone. It's not only healthy, it's a requirement when it comes to self-care. But being alone doesn't mean the same thing as feeling lonely. People who are happy by themselves aren't necessarily lonely. They appreciate their alone time and enjoy their own company. Some prefer to travel alone, some go to movies solo, and many will enjoy an evening out for dinner with just a party of one. In order to lead a fulfilling life, one needs balance. Balance involves a blend of introversion and extroversion. The energy we absorb from time spent with others differs significantly from the energy we experience when alone. Spending time alone allows us to understand who we are as individuals, as well as encourages us to think critically about our values in the world. Focusing on the importance of our time alone, and valuing that time, allows us to allocate our time in a manner that fits our values. It encourages us to choose wisely, as that time is precious.

Your divorce opens the door to freedom on many levels, and your new-found singlehood also allows you to date freely, without commitment, guilt, or obligation. Having said that, as uncomplicated as deciding when to date after a breakup may be, the decision to date specifically after divorce, although unequivocally personal, isn't always simple.

We know that the key to a successful divorce is creating an environment of peace. Although your marriage may have been over for years, assuming your spouse will wholeheartedly approve of you dating may be a little naïve. If you are going to date prior to your divorce being finalized, it is wise to be discreet. It's important to keep in mind that as amiable as your relationship with your former spouse may be, once it is discovered that you are dating, amicable can move very quickly into acrimonious.

Depending on where you are in the divorce process, the decision to date may have a negative impact on legal proceedings. It is always wise to consult with your attorney regarding whether your state falls under "Fault" or "No-Fault" divorce, and the ramifications legally that you are exposing yourself to in deciding to begin dating. Having said that, even if you are divorcing in a No-Fault state, that does not necessarily mean that your decision to date isn't without risk.

Shelly, a former client of mine, started coming to therapy to focus on her newfound independence. She had been married for more than 20 years, raised two children, and finally decided that she and her husband were more like roommates than intimate partners. Her divorce was amiable, but since it was a long-term marriage, the allocation of finances was more than just a little complicated. Since she had been married more than 10 years, her husband would be paying spousal support, to which he more than willingly agreed. She had been separated from her husband for two years and was finally ready to date. They lived in separate homes at this point, so she felt she could do so discreetly. She had begun seeing one man in particular, and felt she was ready to become intimate with him. One evening, while she and a man were sharing an intimate moment in her living room, her husband, who apparently still had a key, stopped by to drop off a piece of mail he had received by mistake. He had not known she was home, and had taken both of them quite by surprise. "It was awkward," she said, "but not as uncomfortable as I thought it might be." That was until the following Monday. She received a rather lengthy email from him stating that because she was now dating, he would be discussing with his attorney a reduction in spousal support. Technically, one really doesn't have much to do with the other, but that does not mean that he was prohibited from bringing up the issue in court. She was shocked. Everything up until that point had been smooth sailing, agreeable, and peaceful. He was hurt and jealous. Although both knew they would not be getting back together, that wasn't enough to stop the hurt feelings from occurring. And, more often than not, it is through the use of a financial weapon that many divorcing people seek vengeance. Her divorce dragged on for another 6 months, exactly 6 months longer than it should have. Although unfortunate, the positive was that her date that night was not only patient and understanding, but in her words, "a real keeper," and worth every penny.

As in anything else, there are healthy and unhealthy reasons for dating and often the unhealthy reasons, as in moving too soon without really knowing what you're looking for, can lead to disappointment. We are social beings, thriving in social acceptance. When socially rejected as a consequence of a breakup or loss of love, we often seek the social acceptance of others. We want to fit in or be accepted somewhere, and often this might involve falling into the arms of the wrong person. Moreover, the tendency to seek a replacement of another, although often unconscious, creates a new risk factor when beginning to date.

Research has found that feelings of attachment can unconsciously transfer from an old relationship partner to a new person when there is some degree of similarity between the two individuals. This transference, although feeling very real and tangible, is merely our mind blending the two, thereby mislabeling feelings and motivations. Brumbaugh, C. C., & Fraley, R. C. (2015). Too fast, too soon? An empirical investigation into rebound relationships. Journal of Social and Personal Relationships, 32(1), 99–118. https://doi.org/10.1177/0265407514525086

Regardless of the length of your last relationship, there is always a certain amount of time needed to not only heal wounds, but to also have personal closure with your relationship. Jumping from the frying pan directly into the fire is a recipe for disaster. People who date prematurely, immediately on the heels of a breakup often set themselves up for continued heartbreak. If the wounds are not healed, then beginning to date too soon will only further delay the healing process.

If you're anything like me, the idea of a new relationship right after my divorce just seemed like one more thing I needed to do. Strangely enough, at least in the beginning, it didn't enter my mind. My "to do" list was so long. But suddenly, when that list eased up, I started thinking about really wanting to meet someone again. I wasn't really ready for a relationship, at least nothing long term. But I did want to meet men my age, who were interesting, and appealing to me. I was curious about my "type" and whether it had changed. It had to have, right?

To clarify, there is a significant difference between dating to date and dating with the desire to be in a relationship. And contrary to what many people think and say, dating can and is fun, depending on the goal. Is it the means to the end, or the end to the means?

When making the decision to begin dating, it's important to check in with your intention and motivations for dating. Try asking yourself these questions:

Can you be alone without feeling lonely, and do you feel satisfied as a single person?

Why do you feel you are ready to date?
What are your expectations?
Do you have the time to put into dating?
How do you handle rejection?
If dating is too much, can you take a time out and focus on yourself?

After you are able to put some time into assessing and determining your "readiness" to date, it's then important to take a look at your level of experience in this world. Depending on the length of time you were married, chances are, the world of dating resembles very little of the world you remember.

Do you have a plan? For example, have friends wanted to play matchmaker, have you noticed or been attracted to anyone in your social circle, are you looking more at utilizing modern technology, or all of the above?

Do you know your boundaries and do you feel comfortable setting them? For example, if you are wanting to be monogamous, can you stand your ground when presented with a friend with benefits situation? Do you know how to stay safe in a sometimes-unsafe world?

Many of us throughout our lives have had some kind of checklist that describes the person we are looking to date. Physical attractiveness, sense of humor, intelligence, they are all on that list. There is nothing wrong with that. But it's imperative that we be realistic. By realistic, I don't mean we should settle. But it's important to recognize that you aren't the same person you were before you married, or even during your marriage. You have indeed changed, and so have your needs. To say that you want the same traits in a person that you did either 5, 10, or 20 years ago isn't realistic, you aren't that person anymore. If you're looking for a good fit, start by making a list of all of the traits you are looking for in another person. Then take an inventory of your own qualities and attempt to "be the person who has the same traits you desire."

When I met Julie, I knew her goal was to have a relationship and she felt she was ready. She had never had a serious relationship, only casual dates with guys she called, "Flaky, selfish, jerks." Her experiences with men who essentially broke her heart, left her bitter and angry, and afraid of putting herself out into the dating world. Realistically she knew she needed to date to find the right guy, but the idea of putting herself out there, only to be rejected, terrified her. She had experienced much loss in her life and had done the therapeutic work necessary to overcome this loss, and maybe she was ready for a relationship. But her judgment was thick. She desired a "certain type of guy," and the bar was high. She was a funny, intelligent, thoughtful, and generous woman. Although these were the traits, she valued in herself, they were not the traits she was looking for in a mate. Physical appearance was high on her list, as was masculine, athletic and successful. Anything less than that was poised for judgment. Unfortunately, she did not find herself attractive nor was she comfortable in her own body. Therefore, the judgment she had for the men who didn't meet her criteria of attractiveness and appeal, was her own projection of herself. She judged herself, her body in particular, and downplayed all of her strengths. She wanted to be accepted in society based on appearance, so she looked for that in a partner. The problem was that when she found it, found that guy who had those traits, she resented him. Not only was she not able to have a connection, she was left angry and disappointed in thinking that she was destined to be single, and she'd never find a quality guy. The problem wasn't quality, it was the lens she was looking through.

Modern Dating Culture: The New Organic

Ideally, I think we would all prefer to meet organically or naturally within our everyday environment. In line at the grocery store, or at church, or maybe while taking your pup out for a stroll. But, relying solely on this as a plan to "date" is basically throwing your hands up to fate and saying, "I leave it up to you mother nature." Maybe because I like a little more control, I've never been one to completely trust fate with aspects of my life that matter.

I met my first husband on Match.com, in 2003, when it was on the cutting edge of online dating. I had experienced speed dating, been set up by friends, and even dated my neighbor, which had been an extremely unwise choice in the end. When people asked us how we met back then, we stammered and made jokes about meeting in jail, or traffic school, because the concept of online dating still felt like we were placing an ad in a lonely heart's column. The reality is that thoughts regarding dating culture have evolved over the countless years of courtship and will continue to do so down the line. And since 2003, the world of dating has evolved whereby what was considered inorganic 20 years ago, is now the new "normal."

In a nutshell, the way a dating application (app) works is by setting up a profile with photos and a description of yourself, but choose your applications wisely. There are hook up apps and dating apps. Some apps are free, and some charge a monthly subscription. Make sure you make a choice based on your goals. Do a little research in this area, read some current reviews regarding dating apps that are more successful than others. Get a feel for what is deemed a "hook up" versus dating and create a plan accordingly. When saying "hook up" by no means am I passing judgment. The idea is to make a choice based on what you are truly looking for when it comes to exploring the world of dating post-divorce.

Be prepared to receive what you put into it. If you put in minimal effort, expect to receive that in return. Put your best foot forward and avoid describing your traits. Use stories or examples to illustrate your humor or your hobbies. Just saying you have a good sense of humor really doesn't give a person the idea of that humor, nor does it separate you from all the others out there who are saying the same thing. Something to the effect of, "I always forget to bring a bag into the grocery store," or, "words like north, south, east, or west, confuse me," gives an idea of humor as well as a little authenticity.

It also gives you the opportunity to feature aspects of yourself that you may have been working on or you are proud of. You could have gotten a new hairstyle, a new outfit, or just started a new hobby. Whatever you may want to show off in your profile photos, you have the opportunity to do so, within reason. Think about how much of your personal life you want to share with someone you haven't met yet. Pictures are important, but it's also wise to consider what you feel comfortable displaying. If you have children, do you want to talk about them in a dating profile, or include pictures? It's a delicate balance when it comes to making choices based on wanting compatibility and also sharing too much, too soon.

Be Mindful of the Paradox of Choice

In a world where there are millions of people, all looking for love, the term "paradox of choice" becomes salient. And in the world of online dating specifically, the paradox of choice is inevitable. In theory, we think it's best to have many choices. We think these choices will surely allow us to find the perfect outfit, the ideal car, or even, the most compatible date.

In Western society, the paradox of choice is a common occurrence. Every day we are presented with seemingly endless options. Just last week my colleagues and I went to a local restaurant for lunch, and my menu was literally 11 pages long. How could I possibly decide on a meal? It took me literally 15 minutes to choose and at that point, nothing looked appealing.

In a world with so many choices, the law of scarcity is virtually non-existent. It is easy to become consumed with wanting the "best of the best." We fear that something better might be just around the corner and if we choose the first item, or even the person we see, we might miss out on something better.

Based on my own personal experiences in dating, as well as the feedback I get from my clients, the paradox of choice can create significant problems. In scanning the profiles of potential dates, because we know we have so many to choose from, we often tend to quickly dismiss potential connections as we hold out for something better. As our fear of missing out becomes more prevalent, our level of judgment increases and we become pickier and pickier, to the point that, in the end, no one looks appealing. There are many, many single people on dating apps, someone for everyone. At times, more often than not, this can be overwhelming, which is when dating burnout can occur.

Let's Do This Right

Anytime we put an effort into a connection, we become invested. Our time is valuable, so the effort we extend immediately becomes an investment, which then increases the value of the person on the receiving end of our efforts. If that connection isn't reciprocated, the loss can sting more than just a little. Although, technically, it isn't truly a loss, the feeling doesn't register the logic, and feels very much like personal rejection.

In a world of meeting one another online, one would think that because there is no face-to-face interaction, rejection would be a non-issue, thereby promoting the comfort that many desire while recovering from a divorce. Unfortunately, in reality, rejection doesn't discriminate. Meeting someone electronically provides a hint of anonymity. A protective barrier if you will. When people behave in a far less inhibited way online than in face-to-face environments, we call this the "online disinhibition effect" (Suler, 2004). Indeed, the effect may be more prevalent in an online dating environment, where people have not met the person with whom they are communicating. Further, the asynchronous (non-real time) nature of the communication may foster a feeling of distance between people online. One consequence of this feeling of distance is a lack of empathy between people which may lead to total disregard when someone replies to a message. Not everyone behaves this way, but when it happens, the key is to try not to take it too personally, which for many of us, is easier said than done. We don't handle rejection well. Period.

To assist in reducing the effects of the obstacles in online dating, we have to create a structure, rules, or boundaries, in order to protect ourselves and be mindful of our hearts. For example, one common dating rule is that once you become interested in someone, try to see about meeting them sooner rather than later. An interesting phenomenon related to online dating is the idea that the more you engage with someone verbally, without meeting them in person, the more likely you are to start creating a fantasy about what this person is truly like. Without meeting them sooner than later, the likelihood for disappointment on the first date increases. The general unspoken rule is that it's important to meet someone in person within two weeks of establishing an online connection. Anything longer than that starts to create a higher likelihood that A) either one of you will lose interest before you even meet and B) When you do meet, you or your date may have already created a fantasy of one another that neither will be able to measure up to. Plus, unless you are looking for a pen pal, do you really want to continue to just chat via text with someone indefinitely?

Have a plan in place regarding safety, and privacy. This is particularly important if you are meeting someone for the first time, or a complete stranger. Just because you've had a great conversation over the phone, or Facetime, doesn't mean it's wise to let personal safety fall by the wayside. Make sure to let someone know that you are going on a date with someone new and tell them where you are going. This may seem trivial, but it makes a difference when it comes to your safety. Letting your date know that someone is aware of your comings and goings doesn't necessarily stop predators, but it may make a predator pick different prey.

If you are unfamiliar with the culture and the technology, it can be difficult to imagine that any sort of app could create any sort of meaningful connection, but it's important to keep an open mind, especially on the heels of divorce. The people you may date now may present as the polar opposite of your ex-spouse, which may not necessarily be a bad thing. Your "type" has probably deviated quite considerably over the past 10, 20, or even 30 years, so be open to stepping out of your comfort zone just a little.

Try to remember that there's no need to share your entire story on a first date. All too often I hear about cases of oversharing changing the tone of what started as a casual, fun date, to something resembling more of a therapy session.

I remember when my client Sally had just started dating after a semi-tumultuous relationship and consequently, traumatic breakup. She had been with her boyfriend John just over 5 years when she discovered that this love of her life had also been busy being the love of another woman's life for the last 4 years of their relationship. Although she ended the relationship, her decision to do so didn't come easily and her brutal recovery had taken just a little less than one year when she finally felt like she was ready to give the world of dating another spin of the wheel. I suggested at the time that it might be a wise idea to role play what a first date might look like for her, but like many of my clients, she was already ahead of me and within a week of signing up for Hinge, a dating app, she agreed to a first date. It was on a Monday following that first "meet and greet," as she called it, that she and I met in my office. "Well, how did it go?" I asked. "Well," she said. "It was crazy but I feel like we've known each other forever." We talked for hours about our lives, and relationships, and I feel like I just really know him, and he just "gets" me, you know?" Yes, I did know, and thought that this may not necessarily be a good thing. I chose my words carefully before speaking. "Sally, did you talk in detail about your relationship with John?" She looked squarely at me and responded, "Well yeah, I mean we both talked about our exes. I mean, it wasn't just me talking." I could sense her guardedness so I pulled back a little. "I meant no judgment at all, as I'm sure it felt like a strong connection. Where did you two leave it at the end of the date?" "Well, he said he would call me. But I haven't heard from him and it's already Monday. I can't stop wondering if something went wrong, or if I did something to make him lose interest." I could tell that her anxiety had gotten the best of her over the weekend. "Sally, I know it's been quite awhile since you've dated, so this is all new for you. This is the first date you've been on since John, and it feels like you're already attached to this new guy. Does it feel like you may be starting to have feelings for him already?" She seemed to think about this for a minute. I could see some of what I was saying was registering. "Maybe, I mean I've been thinking about him a lot, and it's been tough to focus on anything else." This was my concern. Moving too quickly, "oversharing" too soon, tends to lead to a false sense of intimacy, and creates confusing feelings that are often difficult to understand. My approach with her was empathetic and understanding as this is something we are all likely to do when we are excited about a connection, one in which we've been longing to have. "Sally, your feelings are completely normal and healthy. This is all part of the dating process, a learning curve if you will. I do hope you hear from him but it's also important to pull back and focus on the parts of your life that you've built for yourself. Before you met him on Friday, things were great, and if for some reason you don't hear from him again, your life will still be great. The two of you really don't know that much about each other yet. Not really. It might feel like that but it's impossible to have genuine, lasting feelings about a person within just a few hours of meeting them. Yes, you had a connection, but as far as genuinely "getting each other," that comes with time... and taking things slowly. Intimacy is based on trust, and building trust is a process that can't be rushed. Try not to overshare too quickly, and work on being more in the present. Intimate and detailed conversations about past relationships are better served at a slower pace.

Dating should not only be fun, but a healthy and wonderful way to learn more about yourself. What you like, what you thought you liked, and maybe what you had no clue you liked. I've learned more than I ever imagined I would through my dating experiences after my divorce. Dating is not about recreating your relationship with your previous spouse. It is about finding someone that can make you laugh. It's about finding someone you can talk to. And with the availability of 50 million active users on Tinder, and 12.5 million on Bumble, it shouldn't be difficult to bump into another solo traveler, if for nothing else other than a little human connection.

When I first divorced and began dating, the world of "swipe left or right" was completely foreign to me. I was used to meeting people in person, real people, organically as it has been called, and I was able to determine chemistry right out of the gate. But meeting men digitally was a little trickier, and came with its own learning curve. I insisted on having a phone conversation prior to meeting in person. Although I believe chemistry can only truly be appreciated in person, I also know that anyone can sound intriguing via text, but a phone conversation definitely narrows down those who I might be interested in talking to further.

I was fortunate in that I met a lot of nice men, and for the most part, the majority of them were exactly what they said. I say majority, because as grateful as I am that the world is full of people who are dating for all of the right reasons, I am also very aware that some of them are far from transparent, with a separate agenda kept secret from you.

I remember when I started actively dating, yet was still very cautious and conservative in my choices. It was then that I met Bob on Bumble. He said he was newly divorced, as was I, and much of our experiences were similar. He asked me to dinner for the next evening, to which I promptly agreed. We met at this restaurant bar in our town and had an instant connection. We talked, laughed, and just eased into a very relaxed vibe that felt just natural. After dinner, we decided to get a drink at this local dive bar where an acquaintance of mine was the bartender. It was only a short distance away, an easy walk, so it felt safe. When we arrived, the place was packed. Thankfully my friend saved us a seat at the bar, and we were able to resume our easy flowing conversation. I remember thinking, "Wow, this guy is definitely 'second date material.'" It was at that point that my date's wife walked in. For a moment, I was in shock and didn't really understand what was happening. "Who was this woman, and why is she saying that Bob's her husband?" But when she came at both of us, guns blazing, and promptly called me a "cow" it finally sunk in. My friend, the bartender, stood there open-mouthed, as my date and his wife engaged in some battle that I didn't comprehend. Now, "Wimpy Bob," who seemed so smitten by me earlier, acted as if I wasn't even in the room as he stumbled over his words to apparently "his wife," not his ex-wife, but his actual wife. As I finally realized "Wow, this is really happening," I remember saying to Carl, the bartender, "I think I should go" and he, mesmerized by the floor show, agreed. As I said, the place was packed, and was, well, mortified.

Dumbfounded, I scurried out the door with my tail between my legs, feeling like some scandalous home wrecker, and I called an uber. I'm grateful that in my town Ubers are prompt and easily accessible, and Gerome was only 4 minutes away. As I climbed in the front seat, I immediately began spilling my guts to Gerome, who was engrossed by the tale of my evening. I told him how embarrassing it was, and how I just couldn't believe I got duped. It was at that point he said, "I bet it's their thing. You know, that kinky thing that some people do." More shocked by that possibility than I was about the events that transpired earlier, I burst out laughing. I realized, I wasn't dumb in believing this guy, this was about him, and not me. I truly believe people are good and aren't out for malicious intent. Yes, some have agendas and yes, like me, you might get duped. Who knows what their story was, but I'm sure it was a good one.

Gentle Reminders

Remember the importance of trusting your intuition. As women, we often forget the value of a woman's intuition. Men are aware of it, but we often so easily dismiss it. But our intuition couldn't be more valuable when it comes to entering a new world of romantic possibilities. Be mindful of your heart, as well as your instinct. If an interaction with someone just doesn't feel right, honor that feeling. Regardless of the backlash, at the end of the day, it's okay to risk politeness, to replace it with self-care. The right person, or persons will understand and respect your choice.

When it comes to dating either during or after your divorce, like anything else, it's important to strive for balance. When you begin to date, you begin to become acquainted with a whole new world. But that doesn't mean you should lose sight of the world you're in. One should never be a replacement for the other. Although dating might be a priority, it should certainly not be the most important one. Focus on your own value, and not the value you have with another person.

Keep an open mind and remember that not every relationship is meant to last forever. If your marriage was long term, then the world of dating will be completely new to you. Be flexible and look at dating like you're entering into an exciting world and getting to meet new people. And if nothing else, you might get a glimpse of the "kink" of others, or at least a belly laugh from your Uber driver.

CHAPTER 8

Ready, Set, Relationship

Both marriage and divorce feel like the opposite sides of a heavily weighted coin. The beginning and end of one of the most significant relationships in your life will impact, at least to some degree, every relationship in your future that you embark upon.

After severing ties with a life partner, maybe you thought you'd never make a commitment like that to another. Or maybe you weren't sure, but the trauma of divorce was one you knew you never wanted to experience again.

The fact that you will have to grieve the loss of your marriage, like any other loss, is not one to be taken lightly. Not only do you owe it to yourself to take this time, but you also owe it to the integrity of any relationship you choose to have from this point forward. If you rush into a new relationship before you've fully grieved, you'll struggle to feel the excitement and joy a new love can bring. The emotions of loss, or excess baggage, will dilute the intense excitement one experiences when meeting someone new. If you can't throw yourself fully into a new relationship and allow all of those "butterfly-like feelings" to occur, you are always going to feel somewhat disappointed. We all love the feeling a new relationship brings, so why shortchange yourself by moving too quickly?

Perhaps you've dated people, and have a good idea of what you are looking for, but are still wondering, "Am I really ready?" One's readiness isn't a simple "yes or no" answer. It is one that needs reflection, as well as intention. Not all relationships after divorce last and moving too quickly without really assessing your readiness is likely to be a recipe for a disaster. In order to fully answer the question of readiness, not only will you need to examine your own issues when it comes to identifying what you want but also what you bring to the table when it comes to starting on a journey with a new partner.

I think most of us who have been in the final years of a struggling marriage, have felt like we were truly single for a long time. On more than one occasion, I remember feeling like I was a single mom with a husband. But, even though I thought I had been single for those years, truthfully, I wasn't. I wasn't in the single world, where single people mingle, meet, connect, and get to know each other.

More often than not, even in a loveless marriage, in which one may feel single, the daily toll of that marriage is consuming. Our thoughts and feelings are preoccupied with it. Regardless of the situation, struggling with the dissolution of a marriage is all-consuming. Taking it one step further, talk to any newly separated person and the one topic that consumes their mind is that of either their marriage, or their soon-to-be-ex-spouse.

Be Mindful of That "Rebound Elephant" in the Corner of the Room

The period following a breakup can be challenging for many people. But if one enters into a new relationship prior to resolving their old feelings it is generally assumed that this new relationship is designed to provide comfort in staving off the negative feelings that usually accompany a breakup. The "honeymoon period" that accompanies the onset of a new relationship might also help to push unpleasant emotions and memories into the background, offering a person a new set of ideas and emotions to fixate upon.

In this situation, this new rebound partner is usually thought of, either consciously or unconsciously, as a transitional mate (e.g., Lue, 2012). As many people experience despair and loneliness following the end of a relationship, dating a new person can help tremendously in numbing those feelings through distraction or redirection. Perhaps it isn't necessarily the loss of a romantic partner but the idea of losing a friend, or a companion. For many, the idea of not having that person in your life ever again can feel devastating.

There is no way to prevent the painful feelings that occur after a relationship ends. And in a sense, we must actually feel those feelings in order to grow enough to be a complete partner to another. To do anything different would be a misguided attempt to circumvent a very natural process when it comes to relationships. People who quickly venture into new relationships run the risk of entering into those relationships for the wrong reasons and, as a result, may be at a disadvantage.

Despite the pessimistic views that people tend to have concerning rebound relationships, there is essentially no empirical research on these relationships, nor even an authoritative definition of them. As such, we know little about what kinds of people are likely to be involved in rebound relationships or what functions these relationships might serve. One study examining the possible benefits of rebound relationships found that these connections may help buffer the distress that anxiously attached people experience over breakups (Spielmann, MacDonald, & Wilson, 2009). This supports our understanding that the mitigation of the intensely negative feelings after a breakup can be easily dissuaded by appreciating the company and attachment of another.

However, despite the limited research regarding the usefulness of rebound relationships, I remember thinking about my personal experiences after divorce, and also learning through many interviews of newly divorced people, that I never wanted to be the first woman that a newly divorced man dated after his divorce. I just knew that although it was possible that "Mr. Right" thought he was ready because he had felt single during the ending of his marriage, he really had no idea HOW to be single, and I didn't want to be the first "experimental relationship." I had seen and heard it play out that way on so many occasions, so my gut wasn't having any of it.

Delving a Little Bit Deeper into the Readiness Factor

When it comes to your readiness to begin a new relationship, it's important to remember that your self-esteem should be in tip top shape. Even the best of divorces can negatively impact your self-esteem and the lens through which you view yourself. It's likely that you've been in an unhappy marriage for a while, and this can leave you feeling unsure of yourself and your worth.

If your self-esteem has fallen significantly, you may now doubt whether you even deserve to be happy. And when you do head back onto the dating scene or enter a new relationship, you might feel more anxious about it. This can influence how you behave and how others behave toward you, making it more difficult to form genuine connections.

And let's face it, you might experience lots of false starts before you find the right person. This can lead to frustration, disappointment, and uncertainty. All of this can and will weigh on you and make it even more difficult for you to relax and come out of your shell.

For many of us, the ghosts of our past can sometimes confuse or scare us when it comes to new relationships. And being newly divorced certainly doesn't assist in exercising these troublemakers. The term "failed marriage" is one that is used commonly and has damaging effects on the psyche of the newly divorced woman. The implication in this distorted message is clear: the marriage didn't fail, the partners failed. The inverse of this is also disturbing. Apparently being able to stick it out in a marriage that sacrifices your physical and emotional well-being, at least according to society, is a measure of success. Many newly divorced women are already struggling with fear of failure without society adding its two cents and adding fuel to the fire.

Even without the judgment of society, it is common to worry that no one will ever want to commit to you again. You may even fear you've missed your one and only opportunity at partnering up for life. You may feel the impact of harmful words that might've been directed at you, and question why anyone would want you. You might also have lost a little faith in your ability to be a good partner, due to the fact that it feels like forever since you've had an "actual partner." Many of us are familiar with the term "loveless marriage." If this was your experience during your relationship then chances are you are a little out of touch regarding the connection and intimacy that comes with a healthy union. I remember feeling more than a little uncertain at times when it came to my confidence in being an actual partner to another. I had become so used to just relying on myself, sleeping by myself, participating in life by myself, that at times I was unsure in my ability to share parts of my life in a healthy way with a partner.

I also recalled my dating history prior to marriage, which didn't help much when it came to self confidence in relationships.

Prior to getting married I was what you would call a "serial monogamist." I had had 3 long term relationships, which ended up not working. I knew I was immature at the time and although it felt as if I was the one choosing my partners, it was more likely that I was just allowing them to choose me. Perhaps I did this in my marriage as well.

According to research, apparently, we learn more about ourselves while in relationships, than we realize. Ty Tashiro and Patricia Frazier examined the frequency and correlates of personal growth and distress after romantic relationship breakups in a piece entitled "I'll Never Be in a Relationship like That Again." The study discovered self-reported growth among women to be common, as women believed such growth might improve future romantic relationships.

Moreover, participants reported measurable growth specific focusing on how to improve one's own characteristics, traits, and beliefs following a breakup. Tashiro and Frazier note that most of the reported changes were not broad, trait factors, such as being more extraverted, but instead, reflected changes in specific behaviors or attitudes, such as "learning to admit when I am wrong."

It's important to remind yourself that you have changed since the last time you dated. You've grown as a married person, as well as a single woman, and your ability to heal from the process of leaving your married life has assisted in your growth. It's imperative that you recognize that you have learned precious lessons through your personal growth after your divorce, and you are not the same woman you were back then. It is through this growth and allowing yourself time to be the best version of you that you have become stronger and more aware of what your standards are. No more settling.

You're also re-learning how to be in a committed relationship, how to get to know someone and allowing a significant other to start to get to know you. This person doesn't feel your insecurities, they just want to know you. Your first serious relationship after a divorce helps you understand where you're at emotionally, and it will give you plenty of other insights. After your divorce, chances are your standards for a partner have become higher, not lower. Starting a serious relationship will put those standards—and your willpower to enforce them—to the test.

Trust is critical in every relationship. Your marriage may or may not have ended in betrayal, but it is common to feel a sense of mistrust when any long relationship ends. You trusted your ex-spouse and the strength of your marriage and relied on both to be a constant in your life. Whether the choice to divorce was yours or your partners, your trust might now be fractured.

When it comes to a violation of trust or betrayal, it is human nature to immediately become guarded. You don't want to get hurt again and you will do whatever it takes to prevent that outcome from occurring. The problem is, we really don't know how to protect ourselves from heartbreak. Instead, we put up walls all around us, and typically block out all options. These trust issues will not only impact a new relationship; it also impacts your relationship with yourself.

I remember feeling "dumb" when I didn't realize sooner that my ex-spouse had a substance abuse problem. I knew I couldn't trust him, that wasn't necessarily the problem. The problem was that my faith in myself had waned and my trust in my ability to make a wise choice was fractured. And when it came to considering a new relationship, well that was moot because if I didn't learn to establish trust in myself again, how could I possibly trust another partner in my life?

It's also important to fully assess your expectations. It's okay to admit you have them; we all do. But what are yours? Surprisingly, after a divorce, your expectations might be misguided. You may have low expectations of a partner based on your own experience with your ex-spouse. You may think that they will disrespect you, devalue you, or even betray you because you've learned to expect this from a partner.

Having low expectations of another person may hold you back from committing your heart to this new romantic interest. Entering into a relationship with the fear that you might not get your needs met is likely to become a self-fulfilling prophecy. Try to blend expectations with your ability to have an open mind, giving yourself and others a chance to create a new narrative.

On the flip side, you can enter a new relationship with expectations that are unrealistically high. You may believe that this person will heal you and fill the void in your life that was left when your marriage ended. Although having expectations is natural, be cautious of your expectations and temper them if possible. Entering into a new relationship with expectations that are unrealistic will lead to a painful consequence for both parties. A balanced lens in which to view your new relationship is likely to give this new connection a stronger chance of success.

Along with expectations are mindful choices in partners. Although the world is packed full of options, many of whom might be a great match, there are far more who would not. Are you confident in the choices you make when it comes to dating and your ability to stay focused on what you want in a partner?

The question I ask my clients who are either new to the dating world, or are veterans who may be struggling is, "Do you choose your partners, or do they choose you?" The difference between the two options is critical. Those who merely settle for being chosen often realize that somehow, they "ended up in a relationship" that wasn't necessarily with the person they would have picked in the first place. This "settling" leaves both parties dissatisfied and feeling stuck.

It is important to be mindful of the fact that we are creatures of habit and are comfortable with what is "known" versus what is "unknown." Whether we realize it or not, we are more likely to seek out partners who are similar to past partners, even though our past partners might have been unwise choices. We seek out the familiar, often unconsciously. This occurs more often than not when we enter into a new relationship too soon after the ending of our prior one. Without enough time to heal, and process our thoughts and feelings, and begin to understand why our relationship didn't work, we are more likely to choose a partner much like the one we just split from.

After a breakup, we often say that we will make sure to make a better choice the next time. Perhaps we plan to seek out someone very different in order to ensure that we don't end up in the same situation once again. The problem is without the knowledge, insight, and self-reflection that only time can provide, you may think that you are breaking the patterns of your marriage and starting fresh by dating someone very different, but the powers of the unconscious are much stronger than you realize.

When I met Sonia, she had just ended a toxic marriage with a narcissistic husband. Her relationship was emotionally and physically dangerous, and the traumatic impact it had on her left her feeling broken and fragile. The last thing she wanted to do was enter into a relationship with a man on whom she felt dependent. She vowed to "never" make that mistake again. In therapy we worked on finding her voice and practicing boundary setting while working through her traumatic experiences.

She was in therapy for about a year before she decided to terminate based on competing needs in her life. It was about 3 years later that I heard from her again as she was wanting to resume therapy. At that point she was in a new relationship with someone she felt was the polar opposite of her ex-husband. On the surface, her new husband appeared to indeed be nothing like the former. However, he happened to be ill both physically and mentally and needed significant care from her. Although he could financially afford a caregiver, he wanted help from his wife only. He was uncomfortable with her leaving the house without him, yet, more often than not, unwilling to leave the house with her.

Many of the feelings Sonia was reporting were quite similar to the ones experienced in her past marriage. Although her second husband wasn't abusive, she was feeling manipulated and stuck once again. She wondered how she ended up in essentially the same situation once again. She had tried so hard to avoid being dependent on a man, yet here she was once again, feeling stuck and powerless. Although Sonia believed that she had waited ample time in between relationships, her wounds instilled upon her by her ex-husband hadn't had enough time to heal and her unresolved issues were carried into her new relationship. I explained to her that these rebound relationships have a way of filling a gap left by a former partner, whether emotional or practical. For some people, this process might be somewhat symbolic and unconscious. Research has found that feelings of attachment can unconsciously transfer from an old relationship partner to a new person when there is some degree of similarity between the two individuals (Brumbaugh & Fraley, 2007).

How Do You "Make this Work... And Do You Really Need To?"

Those of us who are relationship ready typically can't wait to meet that "right person." This doesn't mean that it is a requirement, but the idea of sharing our life journey with someone is one that elicits excitement and hope. And then that moment comes when you find someone you want to get serious with—and to your surprise, they want to get serious with you, too. Woo hoooo!

It doesn't have to be any more serious than deciding the relationship is official, or possibly exclusive, to give you plenty of new emotions to deal with. Just the words "boyfriend or girlfriend" can be enough to send one's heart and head into an emotional tailspin. Seriously, when was the last time you experienced the beginning of a new relationship?

Five years? Ten? Twenty? And who did you last experience it with? That's right, your former spouse. Try to breathe and don't panic. A little bit of fear is a healthy response. This is all new, and, regardless of whether it's bad or good, adrenaline loves "newness."

Doubting your own judgment, or even the questioning of one's personal right to happiness can make one feel like they're on shaking ground in a new relationship.

When Alana met Paul, she had been divorced for just over 2 years. She felt she was ready for a long-term relationship and decided that she not only could be committed but also couldn't imagine not being committed to him. While in my office, she and I discussed her plan for her to have the "exclusive talk" with him. We decided to roleplay, with Alana being herself and I of course, was Paul. Alana, "So, I was thinking about us, and well, I'm not saying I want to be your girlfriend but was wondering where you saw this going?" Although I knew she did indeed want to be his girlfriend, her statement gave an entirely different impression. I said to her, "So you don't want to be his girlfriend?" I knew of course that this wasn't the case, but it was important for her to realize the risk in this approach and how it might sound to his ears. "What if he just listens to your words and believes that you don't want something more serious. And what if he does want something more serious? You might actually lose him because you were afraid to ask for what you want." This wasn't something she had thought of. Her self-doubt coupled with her keen ability to undervalue herself prevented her from imagining that he too might want to be exclusive with her. Fear and low self-esteem were prevailing, and her disclaimer said it all.

A Word on Vulnerability

The earlier you are able to recognize, understand, and then verbalize your needs to your partner, the closer you become to appreciating and accepting your authentic self. More often than not, if we wait until we are 100% comfortable with expressing our needs, we've waited too long. By staying silent, we set a precedent and create the belief that all is fine. When we finally choose to speak up, our partners are often surprised and thrown off guard. Our avoidance isn't really fair to them either. Keep in mind that there is nothing wrong with asking for what you want, especially if you'd like to give another person the chance to meet that need. Recognize your feelings and be honest about them with your partner. This not only gives space for your voice to be heard but gives your partner room to be honest with you as well.

Yes, this is the first person who you've been interested in having a serious relationship with since your spouse, but they're not the last breathing person on Earth, and being alone beats being in a bad relationship every time. If this amazing person walks away just because you used your voice, they weren't "all that" anyway.

It makes sense to be cautious, after all, you've learned to look for and recognize plenty of red flags, but if you find yourself being too cautious with your new partner, try to challenge yourself to be a little vulnerable. My fear of being vulnerable never truly goes away, but the empowerment I feel when I push past that fear, is what emboldens me to move forward in my relationships. Yes, it's difficult to open up to someone new after a divorce, but until you can be vulnerable again, you will be missing out on the fulfilling relationship that you deserve.

Take it One Step at a Time

Remember that it doesn't have to be a race to the finish line. Yes, your connection is incredible, you understand each other, and you both want the same things out of life. You can't believe you found such a unicorn amidst all the craziness that is the dating scene. You're feeling lucky, and you want to hold on to that luck tighter than one holds on to a winning lottery ticket. But you owe it to yourself to make sure you're not moving too fast.

Perhaps you are so excited that you have found a new soulmate, and based on your perception of time lost, you find yourself moving quickly in this one. In working with my clients, rarely have I heard them say that they moved too slowly in a relationship. But the times I have heard them say that they moved too fast would be too many to count. The problem with moving too quickly, is that the need to slow down has the potential to create a fear of pulling away in the eyes of your potential love.

When my client Marcella came to therapy, just three months into what she called the relationship of a lifetime, she was stressed and distraught. She and her love, Paul, had decided to move in together after dating just two months. She said that they both just knew it was right. So she gave up her apartment, put her things in storage, and moved right in. After what she thought was a blissful month of cohabitation, Paul sat her down and shared his concern that maybe they move in with one another too soon. She said she felt like she had just been hit by a truck. Her head was spinning with thoughts like, "Did he not love her anymore? Was there someone else? Was this over?" As much as he could reassure her that he indeed still felt the same, she couldn't help feel the pain of rejection. I explained to Marcella that other than his expression of concern that they moved in together too quickly, there was no evidence that his feelings for her had changed. The problem with moving too quickly, and then needing to pull back, is that it feels just like rejection. Had Paul said after a month of dating that moving in with each other felt premature, Marcella would have completely understood. But the fact that they moved quickly, with Paul then suggesting reversing their decision, is where the pang of rejection and fear took hold. This was a delicate situation that needed considerable reassurance and trust, which is a challenge in a new relationship.

Allowing a new relationship to grow takes time. In addition, allowing your relationship to move forward at its own pace, or one in which you are comfortable, affords you the opportunity to pay attention to any potential red flags.

Measure your relationship progress by your own internal compass. Are you moving in the right direction at a comfortable pace, or are you accelerating blindly without making sure there isn't a cliff straight ahead?

Sometimes a relationship that moves too quickly also compromises your new found independence. Try not to lose yourself in this new relationship. Remember the hobbies and the new life you created. Although it can be tempting to share every waking moment with your new partner, your personal growth and the life you created post divorce is valuable, and losing sight of that because of a new relationship can send you whirling in the wrong direction. Plus, doing so can often backfire and create a relationship of enmeshment, versus a healthy attachment. Without having separate lives to add to a relationship, an otherwise good relationship will fizzle out quickly.

Based on my work with couples, common relationship issues vary, but some are more common than others, and there are certain common complications that can make a new relationship a little tenuous at times. Communication, ex-spouses, finances, and children; these are the big-ticket items when it comes to post-divorce, relationship hurdles.

It might sound like a simple issue, but communication is more of a problem for most couples than you realize. Many of us think, me included, that we are great communicators. The reality is that most of us communicate poorly, more often than we think. We think that the key to communication is the ability to effectively get one's point across in a manner that facilitates understanding. The fact of the matter is that effective communication isn't about talking at all; the best communicators are the ones who spend more time listening than talking. It's when we truly listen that we can hear the concerns and questions of another, and respond accordingly in order to address their needs.

When we spend too much time talking, we also assume that others are listening, which is often an inaccurate assumption. Pay attention to your partners words, their body language and see what you can learn. Listening is different from hearing. Hearing occurs, automatically, through the use of our ears. Listening takes effort and concentration. Often, most of our time is focused on formulating our response while a person is speaking versus actually actively listening to what they are saying by paying attention to not only their words, but also their facial expressions and body language. And given that words only convey about 7 % of what we are trying to convey, one's facial expression or body language can't afford to be ignored, especially when it comes to a significant other.

Divorces can be messy, and their lingering effects can easily trickle into a new relationship. At the onset of a new relationship, it's critical to tackle any unresolved or even unresolvable divorce issues that are still occurring. Much of this may be out of your partner's control. I've had many clients report ongoing problems with the ex-spouses of their significant others with many of them handling complicated situations in less than desirable ways. Perhaps, in your opinion, the ex-spouse maintains too much contact or too much control. As much as this is disturbing and invasive, it's important to understand more about the dynamic and how much of this is truly within the power and control of both of you. If your partner happens to be a father, as is often the case when an ex-spouse maintains contact, communication between the two regarding expectations and privacy is critical. As much as boundaries are important here as well, complicated situations often require more attention than just boundary setting can achieve.

But sometimes what appears to be a problem with an ex-spouse, isn't always the case. Over the years, my clients have consistently shared stories about their new partners being too accommodating or conceding too easily to their ex-spouses. This tends to infuriate them as they see behaviors such as these as either co-dependent or suspicious, raising the question in their mind, "Is there something else going on here?" But really, what is the real issue here? Is it really about the ex-spouse, or is it more about their own insecurity in this new relationship? Is it a problem within the construct of the old relationship, or one manifesting in this new one? As we know, for every unhealthy relationship is a healthy one in which neither person wants to come in between their ex-partner and a new love interest. Not every ex-spouse has the goal of sabotage on their mind. So, what might look like a red flag, might very well be stemming from your own insecurities.

The first step in tackling these questions is to attempt to understand why this situation bothers you so much. Are you giving too much power and control over to the other person when it comes to your own life? Separating our own issues from those of others isn't always an easy task but one in which you owe the time, energy, and effort to put into exploring, for the sake of your new relationship. These issues often surpass the mere emotional threat of an ex-spouse.

Children can also create complications. Adult kids, younger kids, and anything in between. We love them, but they can create relationship disagreements that can quickly grow into an all-out battle between partners.

When my client Monica met her new partner, Paul, she was nervous. She liked him a lot. He was different from her ex-husband, but still shared many similar qualities. He had two children; one was in college and the other was still living at home but in high school. She had a 13-year-old son. Their family lives were very similar, they shared and appreciated the same intellectual stimulation, and participated in the same social circles. Unfortunately, they met literally 2 months before the pandemic. Since his children were slightly older, she met them first, but wanted to wait when it came to introducing him to her son. Because of the pandemic, she spent many weekends at their house when her son was with his dad, thereby allowing her to become closer to Paul's children. They liked her, which was a blessing. But their parenting styles were different and being in such close quarters allowed these differences to be quite transparent. It was difficult for her to understand her own boundaries and whether it was appropriate for her to share her opinions regarding how he chose to raise his children. She raised her son with a more "hands on" approach and Paul clearly had a more laissez-faire or carefree attitude regarding his children. After she began sharing her unsolicited opinions regarding his parenting, it didn't take long for them to start bickering. In addition, his older daughter struggled with her own boundaries and saw no problem challenging her father regarding his relationship with Monica. As a result, they both clearly needed to get on the same page when it came to their relationship, as well as the relationship he had with his children.

This is where, once again, communication is key. Monica and Paul really needed to work on their ability to communicate. Thankfully his children were older, so they didn't need a stepmother, nor did she need to share her opinion regarding his parenting. Boundaries also needed to be set, with all parties involved. Thankfully, once they realized that maybe they were spending too much time together with his children specifically, it became much easier for Monica to remain impartial, and for Paul to spend quality time with his children as well.

Many of our "own issues" are established at a young age. And our issues with respect to money and finances are ones that we establish early on in our developmental years. Our parents often set the tone regarding our relationship with money. My parents for example spent every dime they made, so we had no savings. When difficult times hit us, we were ill prepared and consequently became indebted. My parents appeared to do well financially, but I knew we struggled, and I felt the pressure on a daily basis. As a result, I never wanted to have to worry about money later in life. I saved every dime and rarely made extravagant purchases. When I got married, I quickly realized that my spouse at the time was raised with similar financial issues. His parents spent money, but also made money. He was also never raised to save money. But rather than fight to not repeat the pattern of his family when it came to money, he established their similar habits. Sadly, I discovered that he enjoyed spending money at all costs. And unfortunately, when he was laid off, the spending continued, and our debt increased. Upon our divorce we were leveraged to the maximum and forced to file bankruptcy. I was devastated. Getting over the financial burden was an additional nightmare I wasn't prepared to face, but I had to, and I did. As a result, I never bounced a check, was never late on another payment, nor did I accumulate any debt.

Moving forward, when starting my new relationship, the first significant hurdle for me was the issue of finances. How would I be able to ensure my financial future along with the future of my son? Thankfully the partner I chose shared my same values, but our communication needed to be spot on in order to avoid any financial problems moving forward. And I was well aware that the issue of money can be a whopper.

Try not to put too much pressure on yourself or your partner in trying to make the relationship work. Working in a relationship is one thing but needing to try hard very early in a relationship can be a red flag. The sooner you let go of the idea that *this time* it should be forever, the easier it will be to go with the flow and see where the relationship does take you. Without forcing anything, without putting too much pressure on yourself or on your new partner.

It's tempting to want to hold on to the first good partner you find after a divorce, but it's important to note that not every relationship, even the good ones, are meant to last forever. And if it ends, remember that you are going to be just fine. You fear that another loss, or possible rejection might be too much for your heart to bear, but trust me, it's not. You survived the breaking of a marriage, you can survive the breaking of a new relationship. Perhaps that's all this relationship should be anyway, a reminder that you can still do it, and a trial run of how to do it. And if it works in the long run and you're happily ever after, then great. If it doesn't, then that just means that you haven't met the one for you, but this relationship was great while it lasted. And at the end of the day, a good relationship helps us grow interpersonally.

CHAPTER 9

My Favorite Superhero
"The Single Mom Warrior"

"Being a mom has made me so tired. And so happy."

— Tina Fey

When I gave birth to my son, I remember my girlfriend Joanne asking, "How in love are you with your new baby boy?" Immediately I knew exactly what she meant. From the second he was born, I was in complete love with him. Up until that point in my life I think I had been pretty selfish. I was an only child, and really only ever had to worry about myself. That's not to say I wasn't immediately terrified. Everything about being a new mom scared me. All of the unknowns felt like too much for my already exhausted brain to handle. And the idea that his little life was one that I was totally responsible for caused my anxiety to fly off the charts.

I remember reading this meme: "As I cut off the crust from my daughter's peanut butter and jelly sandwich, I swear I can hear her whisper, 'she's my bitch now.'" As I laughed, I also thought, "Yes, that is the total truth." And I am also aware that this handful of a

9-year-old little girl will eventually launch, leave home, only to re-turn a decade later, and move down the street from you so you can take care of her kids. So yes, I guess the meme was spot on. So, as much as we adore our children, motherhood is an emotional chal-lenge unlike any other. And that's WITH a partner.

When I thought of having children, more than a few decades ago, I had no idea what kind of mom I would be, but I never imagined being a single one. Because my Master's and PhD pro-grams were very time consuming, unfortunately I needed to put motherhood off until later in life. So, in the 11th hour, one year before my 40th birthday, I became pregnant. And after that, there was no going back. I remember being told to sleep when your baby sleeps, and I think that's pretty funny. I know of very few new moms who partake in this luxury. As much as I might've wanted to sleep when he napped, I felt compelled to wash bottles, clean up toys, do laundry, and complete all of that just in time to hear him wake from his nap.

When my son was 4 years old, my husband at the time was laid off from his company of 25 years, and along with that loss of in-come, was also a loss of all medical benefits. We had just moved a county over and I was planning on closing down my practice and relocating it to our new town. Sadly, his lay off had put that on hold. This was not the time to close down a profitable business only to start from scratch elsewhere, without a second household income. I didn't panic, presumably because I thought it would be only short term. But unfortunately, the short term turned into in-definite, and he remained unemployed while I became the sole breadwinner. I continued to commute two hours a day and came to terms with the fact that the plan had changed.

I thought because I was a modern woman, I was okay with being the primary breadwinner, and that my husband was content being a "stay at home" dad. I was mistaken on both accounts. Our plan was that while I paid for childcare during my office hours so that my husband could work on his writing, I missed out on four very precious years of my son's life. Meanwhile, his writing didn't come to fruition, and his depression and substance abuse consumed him.

As my resentment grew, I continued to compensate at every corner, trying to mask my guilt and frustration at the same time. I was so sidetracked by my own feelings that I had also lost sight of trying to be the best parent I could to my son.

At the time of our divorce, our situation became further complicated due to the fact that my ex-husband was needing to focus on his recovery from substance use, forcing me to truly be a single mom. I had a full-time private practice to run, in two different cities, and a hellish commute that appeared endless. Somehow, I needed to make all of this work.

To say it takes a village is an understatement. For me at least, the art of "asking for help" was one that I needed to master quite quickly if I was going to effectively keep my head above water, for the sake of my son, and also my own sanity. The problem was that I wasn't "open" to asking others for their assistance. In my marriage, I had handled everything, mostly by necessity. So, asking for help, and then relying on that help, felt very uncomfortable. I didn't want to burden others. The belief was that if I was a burden, then people would abandon me. The fear of that happening, especially during a divorce, was terrifying. None of us want to be "left or abandoned." That fear is at the very core of the human experience. But my fear at the time was more salient, palatable, and one that I needed to get a handle on.

So, I did what any good student might do. I practiced. I started asking a couple of my good "mom friends" if they would like to tag team with pick up and drop offs for our kids. Surprisingly they jumped at the idea, and even offered to pick up my son even when they didn't need my help. The kindness of the other moms not only surprised me and touched my heart, but it also restored a little faith in my ability to be more vulnerable, and to not force myself to "go it alone." The fear of burden was quickly dispelled as I realized they wanted to help, and it made them feel good to do so.

My story may be different, but the narrative is familiar. The female mammal is responsible for the providing and care for the young. She is not the pretty partner; she's the partner designed to blend into the environment, to not be seen, in order to preserve the species. She does the work, behind the scenes, and without the credit. And single moms are a special breed. We can handle the work on our own, but that doesn't mean we should.

Single moms are not a new thing, and according to recent research on married moms (68 %), a sizable percent (24 %) are single moms and the number of children living with a single parent is growing rapidly around the globe. Research also shows that approximately 1 out of 4 mothers are raising their children independently. Translating this into context, about 9 million mothers are living with a child younger than 18 without a spouse or partner. Conversely, only 7 % of dads are raising a child without a spouse or partner in the home. (Pew Research Report, May 29, 2013). One would think that along with these growing statistics, society would also step up and provide the necessary support to assist this growing population of women. But alas, at least in this country, most single moms are, more often than not, self-reliant.

For a single mother, the usual stressors (self-care, life balance, financial responsibilities) increase exponentially, and are magnified when going through a divorce. Over the years, as I have worked with clients, many have relayed the same struggles, difficulties, and roadblocks.

For starters, one of the most common emotional challenges for a single mom is an overarching sense of guilt. For the single mom with a full-time job, the guilt we feel is like a giant blanket that envelopes us. We feel guilty even if we haven't done anything to feel guilty about. We can't attend every game, every practice, every play date all of the time, and we know this. But the knowledge that we know does little to assuage the guilt.

Although the number of women in the workforce has increased to nearly 50 % and men have become more involved in the every-day activities related to the raising of children, single moms' time spent on caring for children has not decreased since 1965. On average, mothers still spend approximately 11.5 hours per week per child. Minikin, R. and Horowitz, J.M. (2023) https://www.pewresearch.org/social-trends/2023/01/24/gender-and-parenting. One would think, based on the research, that a working mom's ability to be a strong contributor to the family income would alle-viate any sense of guilt. Unfortunately, the inverse of this tends to be the case, and the lingering sense of guilt as a result of societal pressure is as strong as ever.

I recall at one point during my divorce my attorney saying to me, "Michelle, although it is commendable that you financially supported your family by working, doing so may not look favor-able when it comes to adequate parenting." In a nutshell, she was saying that because I worked so much, the optics might indicate that I wasn't a good mom. I couldn't believe it, yet I did believe it.

The term "superwoman" is one designed to be a joke. But for most of us, the pressure to do everything is paramount. Often, it is thought that the more you do, the more others expect from you. Maybe this is true or maybe it is an overgeneralization. But the pressure to be everywhere at all times does little to relieve the stress that a single mom experiences. From finding a new "Elf on a Shelf" hiding spot every night for a month during Christmas, to research-ing how to make leprechaun footprints on YouTube for Saint Pat-rick's Day, the only true break we really have arrives once per year:

Mother's Day. That is the one day that is ours, even though we normally share it with our children, going to brunch or doing some fun activity. This doesn't mean that we would necessarily make a different choice, but the opinion of society can weigh heavily on our choices. Just recently, I attended my step-daughters graduation at Berkeley. The fact that the graduation was held on Mothers' Day was surprising as well as disappointing. The lack of consideration for that being our day, blew my mind. Of course we wouldn't want to miss a high school graduation. But in doing so, the one day a year that is supposed to be truly ours, is completely shot, by once again, caring for others.

It seems that societies' stigmas catch single mom's both coming and going. Mothers are criticized if they are too involved and admonished if they're not involved enough. Mothers who work are often made to feel ashamed if they miss a game or practice, while moms who don't work are often accused of being lazy.

I remember the first vacation I took without my son. I recall feeling this intense sense of guilt, and worry. He had just celebrated his fourth birthday, and I was thinking of going on a trip to Hawaii. Having said that, it was a work-related trip, and I knew I needed a vacation desperately as I hadn't taken one in ten years, but I couldn't get past this sense of guilt that made me feel like I was being selfish. It was when my sister, who would be his caregiver during this trip, in all of her infinite wisdom, said "You should go because doing so makes you a better mom." For a second, I couldn't quite understand. But then I realized she was right. A healthy and balanced mom is not only better for me, but ultimately the best mom I can be for my son. But as much as my intuition and objectivity told me to go, my guilt was telling me to stay. Guilt is a powerful feeling, but it is far more tolerable than resentment. I could be a mom, but I didn't want to be a martyr. The fact that my sister was able to give me advice, that she herself struggled in following, echoed the pressure I knew most if not all moms must feel in our society. This validation and relatability was just the type of support I needed.

Because so much time is spent caring for children, splitting that time with another parent is not without its own challenges. As much as we know it's in everyone's best interest for both parents to have their own time with their children, single mom's often feel lonely without their children present. We often wonder "what is happening at the "other house?" What am I missing? Let's face it, unless you have the super co-parent situation in which you are able to be at every event in your child's life including those that are on your co-parent's time, you will be missing some experiences. It's inevitable.

Many single moms have little to no support. We talk about taking the time to go to a therapist, or practice self-care, but if you're a single mom without support, who will take care of your kids while you're taking care of yourself? Even if you are fortunate enough to have family living close by, that doesn't necessarily mean that family members are in a position to assist. Even in the best of situations, more often than not, grandparents experience physical limitations, or even schedule limitations, that can inhabit their role as a helper.

A lack of parental support is a frequent complaint of mom's who are trying to achieve some kind of single life. Once able to tolerate the guilt of "wanting" a single life, the act of having one presents another obstacle.

Jennifer, a former client of mine, enlightened me when sharing her repeated struggles with dating as a single mom. Her son's father, who was physically and verbally abusive, was completely out of the picture, financially and physically, so she was truly on her own. She had been single for many years and had pushed the idea of dating on to the back burner. When she finally decided to give the option of dating a thought, her distress about financial logistics was evident. Her parents weren't the greatest parents, nor were they the best grandparents. They did little to support her or her son, so she was essentially on her own. "Should I ask my date to pay for a sitter? Is that something that's acceptable? Does that make me obligated to him in some way?" The first and second questions I didn't have the answer to, the third was a little easier. "I'm not sure if you should ask him to pay for the sitter, but regardless, you are never obligated to do anything you don't want to on a date," I told her. I think many women struggle with this sense of "obligation" when it comes to dating. It's important to remember that if a man wants to go out with you, he wants to take you out and "woo" you, so to speak. So, let him. There is no quid pro quo. But childcare, for her, was a significant problem. She had her son full time, and they were a complete package. More often than not, her son joined her on her dates because she had very few other options. She often described herself in dating as "he took us out to dinner," referring to both her and her son. Boundaries were complicated and confusing.

One of the first things on a single mom's to-do list that tends to fall by the wayside is "self-care." We all know it's important, we stress that importance to our kids all of the time. But when it comes to our own, it tends to get bumped all the way down to the bottom of the list. We often find ourselves catching up on "tasks" when our children aren't with us, rather than taking the time to embrace a little space. Now, I don't intend to undermine the role of a single father, but in my experience, single dads tend to use their time away from their children as the "much needed break" they deserve. As I think about it, I don't think I've ever known a single mom who fit the stereotype of the woman eating bon-bons on the couch while her kids were away. For most of us, the idea of identifying, much less, attending to our needs, may not feel like an option. But, in reality, it is far more important than merely an option. It's a decision that, if honored, is likely to replenish a single mom's soul. The best Mothers' Day I had was one in which I was asked what I wanted to do, and one in which I gleefully replied, "Everyone leave the house, including the kids, and don't come back until I tell you." Then, when everyone was gone, I set about my day refinishing a piece of antique furniture I had set aside the year before and forgotten about. I listened to my very playlist on Pandora, took over the garage, made a mess, and drank Champagne. I didn't end up finishing the project but that wasn't the point. It was my time to do what I wanted, and that is what I chose. It was my judgment-free zone for just one day. Refreshed and satisfied, I allowed my family back in the house appreciating the space and autonomy they gave me and praising myself for asking for it in the first place.

Even when it comes to medical or psychological care, others in our lives come first. I can't tell you how many times I have received a call from a mom who desperately needed her own therapy, but her needs were ignored as the needs of her child or even husband would come first. I'm not blaming the child or the husband in this scenario. Nor am I blaming the mom, not exactly. I have just seen it so often during initial intake assessments, and it certainly sums up our tendency to "feed everyone in our lives" with little left for ourselves at the end.

As I think about this modus operandi of many of us moms, I am reminded of Veronica, a grandmother who contacted me several years ago as she was wanting a therapist for her grandson. She and her former daughter-in-law were still close as she was a very involved grandmother. I agreed to meet with her and her family to assess the situation further and see if I might be a good fit for the teenager. At the onset, it was easy to see that apparently, he was not informed of the plan prior to our visit. Her former daughter in law was also resistant, and Veronica was in the middle of an emotional mess. Although she was not the teenager's guardian, it was easy to see she was clearly the matriarch of this entire extended family. Her son had moved out of the state, and largely due to feelings of guilt, and she felt obligated to assist in taking care of his familial responsibilities. I quickly assessed that based on her grandson's initial reaction, he would not be seeing me for therapy, but before she could slip out the door, I pulled her aside and suggested that she herself would benefit from therapy. By the look on her face, it was clear that she had not let herself consider this as an option. But when given permission to practice self-care, she quickly agreed and scheduled an appointment for the very next day. Although she was unable to fix the problems within her family, through the work she did in therapy, she was able to learn ways in which she was better able to process her feelings of guilt and thereby release herself from her sense of duty and responsibility to others. She learned that she truly had no power and control over others and letting go of that control allowed her to move forward emotionally by focusing on her needs. Learning to set boundaries while also practicing better self-care also contributed to the creation of stronger and more authentic relationships with all of her family members.

Financial concerns are a challenge that many single mom's face, on a multitude of levels. Even working moms report stressors related to providing financial security to their children. Many of the financial struggles are related to lack of adequate child support. Although the law is clear regarding how much child support needs to be paid based upon one's income, the law fails to address the very problem of "lack of follow through" when it comes to what is owed. Courts are backed up, and although child support needs to be paid, if it isn't, many single moms have little to no recourse in obtaining assistance.

I recall a conversation with a good friend of mine, Jane, who was going through her divorce during the same time I was. She was the mother of three boys, with little to no help from extended family. Our situations were similar but a little different in that the law required her husband to pay child support. Although the law was clear, he owed child support, the only thing she received was a promise that he would pay. He was 6 months behind at this point. When they separated, he had moved in with his parents, who were paying all of his bills. He was in the process of starting a business and informed her that all of his money was to be invested in his "start up." His promise was that he would pay her, when that business made a profit. Because they were not officially divorced, although legally she knew he owed child support, the court could do little to enforce this until her divorce was final. Unfortunately, her only option was to believe him, and maintain a running tab of money she was owed.

In need of money in order to pay bills that wouldn't allow her to "wait" until his business returned a profit, she needed to work more hours. She was also well aware that her salary was considerably less than her male counterparts. The irony was that by increasing her hours, her income increased which made child support moot. She was also cautioned by her attorney to "not work too much" otherwise she might have to pay HIM child support. To make matters even more complicated, since he lived with his parents, her kids were rarely with him. Thankfully her three sons were resilient and learned to take care of one another in her absence. Working double shifts, without childcare and child support, with her young sons needing to be self-sufficient, Jane felt trapped, both coming and going. As much as I would love to say that this was an unusual situation, the likelihood of it being rare is low. Her situation is one which affects single mothers on a daily basis.

In Jane's situation, although she was owed many months of back child support, the likelihood of her obtaining any of it was slim. Since her divorce was pending, according to her attorney, it was in her best interest to keep track and a log of "money owed." Technically she should have been receiving child support beginning on the date of separation. But the court date wasn't set for another six months, so without an actual court order, her only recourse was to keep an ongoing record and hope that in six months, she would receive retroactive payment.

Lack of child support, decreased wages compared to their male counterparts, and expensive childcare, either separately or combined, are three financial obstacles commonly reported by many single moms. According to the U.S. Census Bureau, in 2020, women made 83 cents for every dollar earned by men. Changing the context, since Jane's income was significantly less than that of her male co-workers, it would take approximately 40 extra days for Jane to make a comparable wage. Who was to provide childcare during those extra 40 days she would need to work? Unfortunately, the cost of childcare made that option impossible. Like many of us needing childcare, the decision to do so is based on the financial viability. Should you be working just to cover the cost of childcare, if that's even possible?

All of these struggles beg the question, "How is a single mom to overcome these challenges, or at least come to terms with them?"

Our Superpower: Resiliency

Resiliency is one of the most important qualities we can cultivate. It is the capacity to recover from difficulties and adverse situations. It's the ability to adapt and adjust, both physically and psychologically to significant sources of stress. By definition, you are resilient. You've had to be. Motherhood increases your resilience automatically.

Divorce is considered to be the second most stressful life event second only to the death of a loved one and is one in which requires comprehensive changes to your life and identity. Your ability to be resilient helps you and your children recover, adapt, cope, and move forward into what's next.

So how do we cultivate and improve our resiliency? Building on your own resilience does take work, but thankfully the work is already built you're your skill set. The last thing a single mother needs is another job!

For starters, it's critical to be self-aware. To be self-aware is to know what you are feeling, to have an idea of what you are needing, to know your strengths as well as your weaknesses. To be self-aware takes considerable insight. Think about the times you struggled and how you got through it. Think about your skill set, your coping skills, your resources. Remind yourself of all the difficult times you've faced and imagine the pain and frustration during those times. Then, imagine the forces within you that pushed you forward to overcome. Remember that even those extremely difficult times passed. Maybe not right away, but they passed eventually.

Begin to practice acceptance. The term Radical Acceptance is a term used frequently in therapy, and a therapeutic technique which I rely heavily on. To radically accept something is to accept a situation that is outside of your control without judgment. Fighting reality, termed resistance, tends to delay healing and only increases one's pain. Therefore, when we commit to radically accepting something, we aren't "approving" necessarily, we might not even like that which we are agreeing to accept, we are simply letting go of the resistance.

For example, to radically accept a situation regarding motherhood may look something like this: "I'm so tired and I can't imagine having to go to one more tedious softball game this week.

Sometimes it all feels like so much work." By being authentic in saying what many parents feel, i.e., overwhelmed, exhausted, and maybe even bored at your kids' game, you provide yourself freedom from being perfect, and the myth that all of life needs to be within your power and control in order to be okay.

As parents, and especially as moms, we are often feeling overwhelmed and underappreciated. It's so very easy to fall into a pity party and sit there waiting for life to give us a break. But alas, life is not forthcoming of said breaks when your job is to raise healthy and happy children. But accepting life on life's terms, allows us to take a step back without overthinking or analyzing every situation, thereby removing one more job from our overflowing plate. If we allow our thoughts and feelings to merely come and go, our feelings decrease in intensity, and we free up space to think clearly, and more easily. Ironically, radical acceptance is the first step in the change process. When we allow ourselves to talk about our feelings, from the standpoint of non-judgement, our experiences are validated.

Our ability to think critically is one of our greatest strengths. And when it comes to resiliency, one of the most valuable questions is identifying what is within your power and control. If you are feeling stressed, is there something within your power and control that might help relieve some pressure? Are your own expectations too high, and possibly unreasonable at this point? Is it time to modify or adjust expectations? Maybe it's time to reevaluate patterns and behaviors, even if it's for a short period of time. Change is fluid and constant, and transitions are normal and healthy.

When we are resilient, we are able to channel courage and the ability to make change happen. That is not to say we are in "control," instead, our resilience allows us to be adaptable and to experience change on its terms. The term "go with the flow" is a useful phrase when we talk about being resilient. Our resilience allows us to learn from the past, and to become less stuck in the present, thereby allowing us to move forward in life more quickly. Try to appreciate the small things, the little things that are easily forgotten. These little things create our structure and help us become grounded during times of extreme stress. Recognize that even though the "big" things might feel unsurmountable, the little accomplishments may not be so little after all.

Utilizing your support system by sharing your struggles with friends, or others that might relate, is a critical component of resiliency. As you share experiences with others, notice their strengths, or their ability to navigate the difficult situations life has most definitely thrown at them. Look for patterns of strength in others and pay attention to what has worked or hasn't worked as well for them. When we reflect on our own histories, we are reminded of our resilience, but it is when we notice the resilience of others that we can also obtain a glimpse of hope.

Teaching our children to be resilient is a critical part of parenthood. We do our children a grave disservice if we paint a picture of the world in either rosy or gray-covered glasses. As children are often the victims of divorce and tend to feel the effects far more than any parent would wish, we have a duty to not only protect, but also educate and teach. During divorce children may often feel helpless, lost, confused, angry, or a mix of all of the above.

As a mom, the best way in which to ensure a strong, healthy, and well-adjusted child post-divorce is to be the best role model you can. I know that my son more often than not will not want to do what I am telling him to. I'd love to say otherwise, but then I wouldn't be radically accepting the situation. But even though he may not DO everything I tell him to, he will definitely copy what he sees me do. The best thing I can do for him is to model healthy coping skills, practice acceptance and healthy emotional expression, and continue to maintain and set boundaries whenever possible.

Encourage your children to talk about their feelings and provide a safe and non-judgmental place to explore their concerns. As moms, as much as we know we can't rescue our kids, we sure do continue to try. When they hurt, we hurt exponentially more. We can't protect them from life, but we can arm them with the tools needed to be resilient and to feel empowered. Thankfully, research has shown that with the right tools, support, and role modeling, children are resilient.

According to research, merely two years after divorce, most boys and girls are beginning to function reasonably well again. Happily, as long as it is encouraged, the tendency to "self-right" is strong in the young. And thankfully, through the heroic efforts of parents who foster and role model resiliency, these children are more likely to lead healthy and fulfilling lives. FOR BETTER OR FOR WORSE: DIVORCE RECONSIDERED by E. Mavis Hetherington and John Kelly (New York: W.W. Norton & Company, 2002).

The Art of Co-parenting: Why Can't He Just Do It My Way?

Worrying about our kids is nothing new for a mom. And many single moms experience significant worry over the negative effects divorce can have on their child. But research shows that although kids are generally happier with intact families, it is the extent of the conflict that has the greater impact on the health and welfare of a developing child. Simply speaking, it is not divorce itself that causes the most emotional harm to children, but the extent of conflict between parents that tends to lead to lifelong problems for the child.

During my divorce I remember feeling very confused by all of the terms my attorney tossed around casually, assuming I knew how the whole process worked. Thanks to Google, I was able to keep somewhat up to speed. After filing for divorce, I was informed that I needed to attend family mediation. At first, I was confused again. Why would I have to meet with a mediator if I had a lawyer? I soon discovered that family mediation wasn't about my ex-husband and myself, it was about our son. In summary, family mediation is the process in which you and your spouse meet with a mediator to determine a custody schedule. It is required in California when you become divorced and have children, with the ultimate goal being equal custody between two parents. This is most often based on providing fathers the opportunity to take an active role in their child's life with the idea being that even a dad 50% of the time is better than no dad at all. And I agree, at least in most circumstances. In some situations, one parent may be so toxic that a child is better off without that parent in the picture. Thankfully, this wasn't the case in our situation. It was during our family mediation meeting that I learned more about the concept of co-parenting.

The "co-parent concept," a term created in the 21st century in Italy, is a process whereby two people work together to raise a child. In theory, like anything I suppose, this is ideal. But when it comes to a couple in the midst of a divorce, "co-anything" can feel like a struggle.

Initially the idea of successfully co-parenting felt like a tall order. My ex-husband and I couldn't agree on anything, and now we were expected to make decisions jointly regarding our son? I wasn't quite sure how that would work, or if it was even possible. But I smiled and said "Sure, no problem," since the mediator's suggestion wasn't exactly debatable. Great, now I have another job. I also knew that this new "democracy" was going to be a lot more work for me. I was the one who read the parenting articles, the one who volunteered in his class, the one who set up playdates, the one who tutored, made my son's lunches, and drove him to and from school. And now I would be challenged on parenting decisions? I wasn't sure how that was going to work, and I was quickly overwhelmed, once again.

Because my goal is to be transparent, even though most of my friends, including myself, all brag about co-parenting, sometimes secretly, behind closed doors, we complain about it. We bemoan that it's often not fair, and that dad's messed things up and then we are left to pick up the pieces. What we really want is to be able to make the decisions, because we think we know what's best. We've read the books, met with teachers, asked appropriate questions, and essentially, have more skin in the game. We want fathers to agree with our opinions, and "assist us." I'm not proud of this admission of guilt, on the contrary, I know the role of a father is a critical one, and I know this because I had a "couple of them" in and out of my life growing up. But I also know that we feel the way we feel, and more often than not, most single moms I know are juggling more than their share.

Putting my vulnerable and sometimes territorial feelings aside, and tapping into my therapist brain, I know the benefits of co-parenting are ones' that will last a lifetime. For starters, it allows both parents the opportunity to be equally involved in their child's life. It also allows for more support when it comes to making decisions regarding their child. Children who witness their parents treating each other with respect tend to have higher self-esteem and better social skills. In addition, children who are products of healthy co-parenting tend to have better relationships with both parents.

In addition, not only had I once loved my ex-husband, but I also believed when I married him, that not only was he a good person, but he would be a caring and thoughtful father. I also knew that my son was better off having an active father and cooperative parent in his life. I also knew that starting at a young age, children tend to test and often split parents. I had already seen this on a few occasions and knew the importance of presenting a united front, for our sake and for his. Somehow, since I was now a single mom, I needed to figure out how to make this co-parenting situation work. I knew that the bigger picture, the healthier picture, is that the best decisions are one with the child's best interest in mind, and that what is best for the child is something as close to the original family unit as possible.

Co-parenting

Ideally a collaborative co-parent relationship is the most desired option when it comes to co-parenting in general. Collaborative co-parents work together in making decisions regarding the raising of their children. From creating schedules, responsibilities, activities, etc. the collaborative parenting team covers all bases.

When I met Joanne, I couldn't believe her "co-parenting" relationship. That particular weekend, she was getting ready to go to Catalina for her yearly vacation with her ex-husband, her kids, and his wife, aka the other woman. They were renting a house, as they had for the past 4 years, and also a boat for the grandparents who were joining. As I sat in awe, she explained. "The beauty of it," she said, "is that we both get to spend more time with our kids this way. Neither one of us miss out on the "major life moments" that occur when your child is with the other parent. There's no arguing over holidays as they all spend them together usually, and their children get to have a healthy amount of time with both parents. At first, I assumed she was able to do this because her divorce was amicable. But she quickly dispelled this belief. Initially their divorce was as rocky as they come. He had been unfaithful, and then married the same woman. She was angry and hurt, and her children felt betrayed and abandoned. But, for the sake of their relationships, and with much effort on the part of both parents, and a great deal of child and family therapy, they dealt with their feelings, and moved past the hurt and grief.

The fact that you are divorcing doesn't mean that your child's life is forever damaged. Moreover, perhaps the untangling of you and your spouse's relationship can also create an opportunity to parent "better" than when you were married. As I mentioned earlier, initially the idea of co-parenting with my ex-husband felt like an impossible feat. We had been so reactive to one another when we were together, I couldn't fathom how that could possibly just disappear when we divorced. And truthfully, it was challenging in the beginning. But, moving forward, it didn't take long for us both to realize that we were much better parents separately as opposed to together. Our communication was far better than in the past, and as we learned how to better put "our past issues" aside, we became almost friendly in discussing the best course of action for our son. As a result, much to our relief, we watched our son thrive and shake off the nasty cobwebs that seem to accompany divorce.

Stepping into the world of co-parenting requires a strong focus on the common goal, which is what is in the best interest of your child. Most psychologists agree that maintaining a consistent schedule, including routines, provides children with the sense of security and safety necessary to grow into healthy and happy adults. A set, yet sometimes flexible structure creates less stress, and frees up your child's mental headspace so that he or she can do what they are meant to do, be a kid.

And since structure is critical to the health and well-being of your child, creating a plan is the first step. Your plan should include the basic physical areas of your child's including home, school, extended family, and friends. It should also address the emotional needs, including your child's temperament, strengths and weaknesses, discipline, feelings related to comfort and safety, and how to handle concerns related to reaching out to the other parents when interpersonal issues arise.

Ideally it is helpful if collaborative co-parents work together to determine household rules. Obviously, there's no way to expect that both of you will implement household rules exactly the same but agreeing overall regarding the most effective form of implementing them will assist your child with structure and accountability. Will there be a curfew, chores, responsibilities, expectations? And, if not followed, what are the consequences?

It's also important to include in your plan how to plan for the unexpected. What form of communication is preferred for both parents? How will finances be split when something comes up unexpectedly? Is it okay for one parent to decide on behalf of the other if need be?

Once you've created a plan with general guidelines, determine a schedule that works for your family. Family mediation will provide parental allocation, formerly known as "joint custody," on paper, but it's up to you to create a clearer picture of what works best for your family. Try to plan holidays, birthdays, or anniversaries in advance. Days like those can easily become sources of great conflict, so best to get that out of the way at the start.

However much you prepare, conflicts will happen. And while you can't avoid them, it's important to remember to never lose track of your goal. Whenever possible, try to co-parent as a team. And, as odd as it may sound, try to trust your co-parent. I understand how this may sound difficult, or even counterintuitive depending on the circumstances of your divorce. But try to trust that you and your co-parent have the same common goal, what is in the best interest of your child. Remember that as much as we may think we are right, there is never just "one way" to do something. This is especially true in parenting. If something bothers you about how your co-parent is parenting, try to address it sooner than later. The idea is to address matters in a calm manner, as you would a business partner. Sometimes this entails taking a step back and possibly taking a time out. My recommended baseline to my clients is that if you are feeling angry, stressed, or anxious, and it's over a 5, with 0 being calm and 10 being off the charts, wait until you are calmer and address it at that time. Remember that communication is vital when it comes to successful co-parenting and healthy child development. Listen, compromise, and remember to breathe.

Try to treat your co-parent as you would like to be treated. Support them and consult them on decisions. Mutual respect can go a long way in co-parenting and is one of the best ways to ensure that the process has a higher likelihood of running smoothly. One of the difficult aspects of co-parenting in divorce is reconciling the emotions related to "missing out" on half of your child's life experiences. As much as Simon and I both want our son to experience every possible magical moment of childhood, the fact that we will not be present for all of them is almost heartbreaking at times. However, thankfully modern technology can assist tremendously by allowing us to share these moments with each other. So, take a moment to snap a picture of your child engaging in whatever activity is happening and share it with your co-parent. A kind and thoughtful gesture can go a long way in maintaining trust and rapport, and can also remind your co-parent to do the same.

What to do if you're not ready to co-parent? Examine your resistance and identify whether or not that resistance is based on the reality of the current situation, or the history of your relationship with your spouse. If it's the latter, try focusing on your child and let go of your negative feelings and beliefs about your co-parent. If it's the former, then it's possible that co-parenting collaboratively may not be in the cards for you both at this time.

As much as co-parental support, cooperation, and agreement are positively associated with overall mental health, self-esteem, and academic performance, it isn't without its challenges. While the behavior of an ex-spouse or former partner is out of our control, we do have a say when it comes to our own thoughts, feelings, and actions. Regardless as to how your co-parent might respond, by setting a positive example for your child, your children will notice and build trust in you, all of which increases your influence and place in their lives.

Being a parent isn't just about "collaborating." It's important to remember that even if your co-parent isn't on board with collaboration, you still have a critical job to do, and even if you only have your child part time, your parenting role is significant in your child's life.

According to recent research by Dr. Mavis Hetherington, if there is very little conflict between divorced parents and parenting is loving, firm, and consistent, children can thrive in mother, father, or joint custody situations. For many parents, this newer research provides hope in that we now know that divorce doesn't inevitably produce permanent scars. A good parent can buffer or shield a child from the many stresses associated with divorce and unique challenges faced within a single-family home. Hetherington, E.M. and Kelly, J. *For Better or For Worse: Divorce Reconsidered* (2002) New York: W.W. Norton & Company.

Identify your own values and make rules and enforce those that support your principles. You can make parental suggestions to your former spouse, or discuss parenting ideas, but at the end of the day, if you and he are not on the same page, you will still need to stay focused on your parental values in your own home. Try not to fixate on "how your ex-spouse parents" as, once again, this is

not within your power and control. Keep your emotional and physical energy focused on things that are in your wheelhouse.

Avoid talking badly about your co-parent in front of the children. As a general rule, try to avoid negative talk even if your children are in the nearby vicinity. It's amazing what children hear
when we don't want them to, but what they don't hear when they
are supposed to. When you talk about your co-parent in front of
your children, please do so with respect.

Remember that your child is your child, and not your friend.
Although he or she may feel like a confidant, that is not their role.
Boundaries are very important. As much as you might want to
share with them the fact that you got stuck paying for all of their
soccer expenses, especially if their father told them otherwise, try
to bite your tongue. The immediate gratification is not worth the
longer-term effects that type of information will have on your
child. Unfortunately, children do see far more than we realize, so
adding salt to the wound only makes the wound more painful in
the long run.

I recall a time when I took my son and his friend bowling. His
friend's father was a pro bowler, which impressed my son to no
end. I remember his friend asking him what sport his dad played,
and my son replied, "My dad doesn't do anything." At that exact
moment I thought, "Hmmm, I should feel good about the fact that
my son sees the struggles I faced with his dad" but instead, I just
felt sad, and sorry for the both of them. I wished I could have
spared my son the knowledge he already knew at that moment.

Even if communication is difficult between you and your ex-
spouse, avoid using your child as the messenger. Discuss with
your co-parent the best modem of communication between the
two of you. When children are caught in the middle of two parents who don't communicate, all three lose. It's not their place to
do your job for you. It may seem easier at the moment, but then,

who said being a parent is supposed to be easy? Even in the short-term having your child act as the go-between sets the stage for your children to lose respect for both parents, which is the opposite of what every parent wants.

Remember that your child loves both of their parents, and by openly showing your co-parent respect, your child will grow to love both of you even more.

When I think of my mom, I immediately feel 5 years old. It's crazy that one person can have that much influence over another, and that attachment is at our very core as humans. That's the power of a mother. Good or bad, she is like no other. Her strength, especially during times of struggle, is a reminder that we too have power, and that we truly are, all heroes.

So, mama bear, I say to you, "You've got this, but you're not alone." There's a tribe right behind you.

Appendix

Your Divorce Checklist

Property

Currently, there are nine states (namely, AZ, CA, ID, LA, NV, NM, TX, WA, and WI) that are considered Community Property States in which the law holds that all assets acquired during the marriage by either spouse are considered joint marital assets. These assets are generally divided equally between the spouses in a divorce. Be sure to familiarize yourself with the laws that govern the division of property in your state.

Beyond the unique laws in community property states, there are several other avenues one can take in order to decide the appropriate division of marital property. Although it is possible for spouses to come to a relatively amicable agreement about the division of property, if you are in disagreement about one or more items, there are a number of fair methods for deciding how to divide up property.

One of the most common is bartering, where one spouse takes certain items in exchange for others. For example, the wife may take the car and furniture in exchange for the husband getting the boat. Another method used in the division of property is to sell the marital property and divide the proceeds equally. Often, mediators or arbitrators may also be used.

Dividing Debts in Divorce

Often even more difficult than dividing the property in a divorce is deciding who will be responsible for any debt the couple has incurred during their marriage. In order to do this, you'll need to know how much you owe and to whom.

Whether you trust your spouse or not, I recommend ordering a copy of your credit from each of the three credit reporting agencies: Equifax, Experian, and TransUnion. Your credit report breaks down everything you owe in your name, including joint accounts you share with your spouse.

Go through the credit reports and identify which debt is shared and which is in your spouse's name only. At this point, it's important to stop the debt from growing any larger while you're in the process of getting divorced. The best way to do this is to cancel, if possible, joint credit cards leaving one card in your name in case of emergencies.

Once you've identified your debts and taken steps to ensure they don't increase, it's time to decide who will be responsible for what debt. There are several ways to do this, including:

- If possible, pay off the debts now. If you have savings or assets you can sell, this is the cleanest method. You don't have to worry that your spouse will leave you responsible for his/her portion of the debt, and you can start your new life debt-free.
- Agree to take responsibility for the debts in exchange for receiving more assets from the division of your property.
- Agree to let your spouse take responsibility for the debts in exchange for receiving more assets from the division of property.

- Agree to share responsibility for the debts equally. Though at first glance this choice appears most "fair," it does leave both of you the most vulnerable. Legally, you are still responsible if your ex-spouse doesn't pay up, even if she or he signs an agreement taking responsibility for the debt.

Tax Issues

People sometimes get caught up in the most obvious and talk about issues of divorce such as the division of property and debt, who will have physical custody of the children, etc. As a result, many don't think through the tax implications of their divorce, an oversight that can cost thousands of dollars or more.

This is where a certified public accountant (CPA) comes in very handy as a part of your divorce team. Tax issues that may arise from divorce can include:

- Who will get the tax exemption for dependents?
- Who will be able to claim Head of Household status?
- Which attorney fees are tax-deductible?
- How can you be sure "maintenance" payments will be tax-deductible?
- How can you avoid the mistake of having child support be non-deductible?

Of course, as tax law changes and your unique situation may require special consideration, be sure to also consult a tax professional.

Addressing Social Media

Although you may be mindful of your social media content, the content of others can easily be linked to you as well. When you are in the middle of settling things, social media is being referenced more often now in determining the division of the marital assets, child support, alimony, and custody.

According to the National Law Review, 81 % of divorce attorneys discover social media evidence that is worth presenting in court and 66 % of divorce cases use Facebook as one of the primary sources of evidence. As a result, as a preemptive action, most mediators as well as many attorneys suggest that you agree at the time of separation, to include a personal "Social Media" clause. This arrangement constitutes that both parties agree not to post on Facebook, or tweet on Twitter or any other social media sites, where either party or their respective families could be viewed negatively.

Don't Forget to Address Retirement Plan Issues

If your spouse has retirement savings, you are probably entitled, by law, to half. This money can be used for your own retirement or for a down payment on a house, relocation expenses, or other current expenses. To avoid the 10 % penalty on early withdrawal, be sure to follow IRS regulations. This information can be obtained on the IRS website, www.irs.gov.

The primary issue with retirement assets is that while the assets may or may not have been sufficient for your joint retirement needs, more than likely your individual retirement needs will be much greater. As a result, not only must you consider how these assets will be divided, but how you will continue to contribute to them in order to secure your financial future in retirement (even as your near future may be in question as well).

Divorce can bring out the worst in some people, and you need to be aware that even the most honest of people may try to cheat when it comes to settling up financially in a divorce. Spouses may underreport income, ask an employer to delay a large bonus or salary increase, among other dishonest behaviors. Most vulnerable are those whose spouse owns a closely held business.

The best defense when facing the financial concerns of a divorce is knowledge. It is particularly important for both spouses to educate themselves about their joint finances so that nothing remains a secret to be overlooked. In the case of divorce, ignorance is not bliss.

The "Not So Basics" (10 Things They Won't Tell You Unless You Ask)

1. Whether you will continue to be living in your house or not, obtain a post office box. This is to ensure important pieces of paperwork don't get misplaced or lost. Your ex-spouse will undoubtedly still receive miscellaneous paperwork at your residence, and you might even mix up legal documents during the process. Having a PO box for important documents ensures that every important piece of communication is accounted for.

2. Change your passwords on all of your accounts. It may not feel necessary but it's likely to prevent any confusion or discord in the future. Even in the most amicable of divorces, if one spouse has access to accounts, the likelihood for private communication being discovered can complicate a peaceful situation.

3. If you are a parent, obtain a life insurance policy on your ex-spouse to secure child support payments just in case something happens to him. This is rarely something an attorney will share with you, but it is an issue that comes up more often than you think. Always hope for the best but be prepared for the worst.

4. Splitting every cost child-wise 50/50 may seem like a simple solution at face value but think long term. You don't have to accept a 50/50 ratio and you most certainly can recommend a different one based on your current earning power as well as future earning power. The last few years of this pandemic has certainly made more people re-examine the "assumption" that their income is sustainable. At this point nothing is certain, so keep that in mind when negotiating.

5. Spousal support is negotiable, but child support is not. All states treat both of these separately. Typically, you can obtain a child support calculator to determine what the law will ask for when it comes to child support. However, even if you have the majority of custody, don't assume you will be entitled to child support. This all comes down to who makes the most money and if that income can be PROVED. Remember that it's not about the truth, it's about what can be proved. Many spouses hide income in terms of using parent's name, or altering financial records so be prepared to keep an eye on all bank records and account holders.

6. If you have children, keep a calendar with a log of on-going issues. Note issues with respect to difficulties with scheduling, pick up and drop offs, extra expenditures, etc. Keep record of times that your children were scheduled to be gone, but may have been dropped off early, or when you were expected to cover various expenses that weren't part of your agreement.

7. Avoid maintaining co-ownership of your house with your ex-spouse. Although the idea might appear financially sound, or even in the best interest of any children, there are too many issues that can and will go wrong in this scenario. From a leaky

roof to a spouse who loses his job and cannot pay the mortgage any longer, your financially sound decision will inevitably take a turn for the worst. Talk to your financial planner about options to prevent this situation from occurring.

8. If your divorce appears to look like it will potentially be lengthy or complicated due to child custody or financial issues, research the option of bifurcation. Bifurcation is essentially splitting the aspects of divorce in two separate parts. It allows you to legally divorce, and move on with your life, while still working through any custody or financial complications. Typically, attorneys will not present this as an option as it tends to streamline a financially weighed divorce, thereby reducing attorney fees during the process.

9. If you have special needs that require you to stay home with or without a child, while your divorce is pending, you can ask the court for temporary spousal and child support. Since the divorce process can be lengthy, temporary support can often ease the burden during the process.

10. The most significant message in this checklist is that your divorce agreement can be anything you want it to be. In my case, I knew I made the majority of the income and had 70/30 custody, so when it came to taxes, I wanted to be Head of Household every year. I knew that usually it is recommended that spouses alternate years, but that made no sense to me and thankfully the IRS agreed. My attorney balked and so did my husband at the time, but I stood my ground. I recall my attorney being fearful that my spouse might sue for child support, but for me it was worth the risk. If he wanted child support then he was free to bring me to court and ask for it, and I

would happily post the video on YouTube but until then I was HOH. I felt bullied, even by my attorney, and I was tired of doing all of the right things and biting my tongue based on fear. The message here is that if something doesn't feel right, speak up. Every decision you make will impact the rest of your life, and if you have children, it will impact them heavily as well, so take your time and don't let others rush you into making a decision you aren't ready to make. Everything is emotional and everything feels urgent, but it doesn't have to be that way. It can be on your terms, just take your time and determine what they are, ask for what you want, continue to set boundaries, and believe in yourself.

Readiness Assessment

Check each item in the ten areas below that is true for you. Try to be objective and honest with yourself. We recommend asking close friends and family members for their opinions as well.

I	*My Vision, Values, and Life Purpose*
	1. I have a "Vision" of what I want for my life and my relationship
	2. I am clear about my values and live by them
	3. I have identified my purpose and do my best to honor it
	4. I know how I want to live and know I am responsible for my own happiness.
	5. I am living my life fully and in alignment with my vision, values, and life purpose
	Total

II	My Requirements
	1. I will not allow myself to be talked out of what I need, nor will I second guess my requirements
	2. I know what I can't live without in a relationship and don't settle for less
	3. I know what values I must share with a partner
	4. I am clear about what personality traits and qualities I most value in a partner
	5. I am clear about what interests/activities I must share with a partner
	Total

III	My Needs
	1. I know what I need emotionally to feel loved in a relationship
	2. I ask for what I need and want, and take responsibility for the outcome
	3. I do not expect a relationship to meet all my needs and make me happy
	4. I have a support system to supplement meeting my social and emotional needs
	5. I have inner strength which helps me be self-reliant and proactive about my needs
	Total

IV	My Relationship History and Patterns
	1. I understand what did and didn't work for me in previous relationships
	2. I understand which positive and negative relationship patterns I risk repeating
	3. I am aware of habits, patterns, and values I have inherited from my family
	4. I understand my past patterns of choosing partners
	5. I understand my past relationship attitudes, choices, and actions/behaviors
	Total

V	My Emotional Issues
	1. I have let go of relationships which are damaging to me
	2. I have forgiven people who have hurt me
	3. I am able to forgive myself for my past mistakes
	4. I trust that everyone does the best they can at all times
	5. I am aware of, and own, my emotional issues when they arise in a relationship
	Total

VI	**My Communication**
	1. I clearly communicate what I want and need; I don't make people guess
	2. I deal positively with misunderstandings and disagreements when they occur
	3. I make requests rather than complain
	4. I regularly practice active listening, give validation, and express appreciation
	5. I am careful about what I promise and keep my word
	Total

VII	**My Community**
	1. I am aware of how I come across and affect others
	2. I am surrounded by caring people
	3. I spend my social time with healthy, happy, able people
	4. I take extraordinary care of the people I have chosen to love
	5. I am a member of two or more communities (hobby, spiritual, professional, etc.)
	Total

VIII	**My Lifestyle**
	1. I am satisfied with my work/career
	2. I support my present lifestyle and am preparing for my future security
	3. I have no financial or legal problems
	4. I am living the life that I want as a single person, yet I am available for a committed relationship
	5. I am healthy in mind, body, and spirit
	Total

IX	My Dating Patterns
	1. I take initiative and responsibility for choosing who I want in my life and don't wait to be chosen
	2. I have clearly defined guidelines for sexual involvement that I adhere to
	3. I balance my heart with my head and make careful relationship choices
	4. I do not interpret infatuation, attraction, attachment, and/or good sex as "Love"
	5. I do not expect a relationship to "rescue" me from emotional or financial problems
	Total

X	My Relationship Plan
	1. I understand and use the "Law of Attraction" (like attracts like)
	2. I am clear whether I am seeking a short-term recreational relationship or am ready to seek a long-term committed relationship
	3. I effectively disengage from prospective partners who are not a fit for me
	4. I will not try to convince myself that someone is a fit when they clearly don't meet my needs
	5. I am balancing my partner search with investing in myself and living my vision
	Total

Results

Mark an "X" on the line corresponding to your total score in each section.

	I	II	III	IV	V	VI	VII	VIII	IX	X
6+										
5										
4										
3										
2										
1										
0										

▶ What are your strongest areas?

_____

_____

_____

▶ What areas need improvement?

_____

_____

_____

▶ What do you need to learn more about?

_____

_____

_____

▶ What are the top 5 items that could most interfere with the success of your next relationship?

_____

_____

_____

Thought Record

Date/time	Situation	Automatic Thought(s)	Emotion	Adaptive Response	Outcome
	What event (external or internal) is associated with the unpleasant emotion?	1. What thought(s) went through your mind (before, during or after the event or unhelpful behavior)? 2. How much did you believe the thought(s)?	1. What emotion(s) (sad / anxious / angry, etc.) (did you fell (before, during or after the event or unhelpful behavior)? 2. How intense (0-100%) was the emotion?	1. (optional) What cognitive distortion did you make? 2. Use questions below to compose a response to the automatic thought(s). Indicate how mucho you believe each response.	1. How much do you now believe each automatic thought? 2. What emotion(s) do you feel now? How intense (0-100%) is the emotion? 3. What would be good to do?

Questions to help compose an alternative response: (1) What is the evidence that the automatic thought is thue? Not true? (2) Is tere an alternative explanation? (3) If the worst happened, how could I cope? What's the best that could happen? What's the most realistic outcome? (4) What's the effect of my believing the automatic thought? What could be the effect oh my changing my thinking? (5) If (person's name) was in the situation and had this thought, what would I tell them? (6) What would be good to do?